T0328695

Cambridge Elements ≡

Elements in Eighteenth-Century Connections
edited by
Eve Tavor Bannet
University of Oklahoma
Rebecca Bullard
University of Reading

PHILOSOPHICAL CONNECTIONS

Akenside, Neoclassicism, Romanticism

Chris Townsend
Christ's College, University of Cambridge

CAMBRIDGE
UNIVERSITY PRESS

CAMBRIDGE
UNIVERSITY PRESS

University Printing House, Cambridge CB2 8BS, United Kingdom

One Liberty Plaza, 20th Floor, New York, NY 10006, USA

477 Williamstown Road, Port Melbourne, VIC 3207, Australia

314–321, 3rd Floor, Plot 3, Splendor Forum, Jasola District Centre,
New Delhi – 110025, India

103 Penang Road, #05–06/07, Visioncrest Commercial, Singapore 238467

Cambridge University Press is part of the University of Cambridge.

It furthers the University's mission by disseminating knowledge in the pursuit of
education, learning, and research at the highest international levels of excellence.

www.cambridge.org
Information on this title: www.cambridge.org/9781009222976
DOI: 10.1017/9781009222990

© Chris Townsend 2022

First published 2022

A catalogue record for this publication is available from the British Library.

ISBN 978-1-009-22297-6 Paperback
ISSN 2632-5578 (online)
ISSN 2632-556X (print)

Philosophical Connections

Akenside, Neoclassicism, Romanticism

Elements in Eighteenth-Century Connections

DOI: 10.1017/9781009222990
First published online: May 2022

Chris Townsend
Christ's College, University of Cambridge
Author for correspondence: Chris Townsend, ct409@cam.ac.uk

Abstract: Neoclassical and Romantic verse cultures are often assumed to sit in an oppositional relationship, with the latter amounting to a hostile reaction against the former. But there are in fact a good number of continuities between the two movements, ones that strike at the heart of the evolution of verse forms in the period. This Element proposes that the mid-eighteenth-century poet Mark Akenside and his hugely influential *Pleasures of Imagination* represent a case study in the deep connections between Neoclassicism and Romanticism. Akenside's poem offers a vital illustration of how verse was a rival to philosophy, and promotes a new perspective on philosophic problems of appearance, or how the world 'seems to be'. What results from this is a poetic form of knowing that foregrounds feeling over fact, that connects Neoclassicism and Romanticism, and that Akenside called the imagination's 'pleasures'.

Keywords: Neoclassicism, Romanticism, philosophy, verse, Akenside

ISBNs: 9781009222976 (PB), 9781009222990 (OC)
ISSNs: 2632-5578 (online), 2632-556X (print)

Contents

'By what fine ties hath GOD connected things
When present in the mind; which in themselves
Have no connection?'
The Pleasures of Imagination
Book III, 462–4

Introduction, or 'The Design'

'We have inherited the myth of a radical generic breakdown in European Romanticism that in fact never happened.'[1] It was once the case that Romanticism was assumed to be a great flash of originality within the history of poetry – a wholesale rejection of the preceding generations of verse, one that replaced reason with passion, formal completeness with fragmentation, human society with nature, beauty with the sublime. There was Enlightenment rationality, then there was Romantic imagination. There was Pope and the balanced heroic couplet, then there was Wordsworth and stately blank verse. In each case, the latter is always posited as a reaction against and a rejection of the former. Stuart Curran, in his groundbreaking study of Romanticism's relation to its own literary past by way of 'connotative' designations of genre (the hymn, the ode, the elegy, the romance), suggests that such inherited 'myths' of a break between the Romantic poets and their direct predecessors is a product of Romanticism's own self-mythologizing. The quest for originality of expression is indeed a hallmark of Romanticism, and it is no doubt a product of what Harold Bloom influentially called the 'anxiety of influence' shown by writers and poets towards that which came before.[2] Such an idea is contained in William Blake's statement that 'I must Create a System, or be enslav'd by another Mans.'[3] A century before Modernism and the Poundian maxim to '*make it new*', Romanticism was already promoting poetic novelty by forcing a distance between itself and its recent past.[4]

Curran continues his reflections on Romantic myth-making by observing that the narrative of such a 'breakdown' with 'its own logic of cultural determinism has essentially distorted our perceptions of both Romantic literature and culture'. In what Jerome McGann has influentially termed 'the Romantic ideology', there is a tendency in scholarship towards reproducing in critical writings the very terms and ideals that Romanticism set out to establish – perhaps

---

[1] Stuart Curran, *Poetic Form and British Romanticism* (Oxford: Oxford University Press, 1986), p. 5.

[2] Harold Bloom, *The Anxiety of Influence: A Theory of Poetry*, 2nd ed. (Oxford: Oxford University Press, 1997).

[3] William Blake, *The Complete Poetry & Prose of William Blake*, ed. David V. Erdman (New York: Anchor Books, 1988), p. 153.

[4] Ezra Pound, *Make It New* (New Haven, CT: Yale University Press, 1935).

uncritically so.[5] This matters because even where we might imagine we are reading against the grain of Romanticism's myth-making, we might very well still be reinforcing its alleged split from the eighteenth century. The word 'Romanticism' – not itself a product of the Romantic-period writers but of their subsequent critics – sets into motion the conception of the Romantics as historically distinct within the traditions of literature, and strangely so: 'Romanticism' in modern academia is both an essential hinge and a double misfit, forming the overlapping middle term between eighteenth-century litera- ture and the Victorian period. Thus, it is not quite at home in either of the 'long' centuries between which it falls.

It would be true to say that the narrative of Romanticism as a clean break from eighteenth-century verse cultures has been overturned. There are abundant sensi- tive studies of the debt the Romantics owe to mid-eighteenth-century poets including Edward Young, Thomas Gray, William Cowper, and Christopher Smart, as well as the earlier extra-Augustan poet James Thomson.[6] Yet though it can be imagined that Romanticism owes something to that group of writers who are sometimes even grouped together in survey courses as 'proto-' or 'pre-' Romantics, it remains difficult for scholarship to imagine anything other than a complete rejection by the Romantics of Augustan-era verse, and especially of Alexander Pope. Beth Lau, opening a short essay on Keats's poetic precursors, offers the view that 'the literary movement we call Romanticism was shaped in significant ways by a rejection of Augustan and celebration of Renaissance poetry and aesthetics'.[7] The view is familiar and it is backed up by the abundant evidence that Keats admired Spenser and Milton but did all he could to 'get as far as possible in the opposite direction of the Pope school'.[8] It is demonstrably true that Keats's poetry in particular was responsive to Pope's poetry and what Keats, under the influence of Leigh Hunt, would label the 'rocking horse' poetics of the Augustan heroic line.[9] Such a response was in the spirit of Romanticism more broadly, with Wordsworth's remarks against 'poetic diction', in the celebrated 'Preface' to his

---

[5] Jerome J. McGann, *The Romantic Ideology* (Chicago: University of Chicago Press, 1983).

[6] Such studies often place Wordsworth at their centre as a lynchpin of high Romanticism. See, for instance, Tess Somervell, 'Mediating Vision: Wordsworth's Allusions to Thomson's *Seasons* in *The Prelude*', *Romanticism*, vol. 22, no. 1 (2016), pp. 48–60; Stefan H. Uhlig, 'Gray, Wordsworth, and the Poetry of Ordinary Life', in *The Meaning of 'Life' in Romantic Poetry*, ed. Ross Wilson (New York: Routledge, 2009), pp. 33–56; Tim Fulford, 'Wordsworth, Cowper and the Language of Eighteenth-Century Politics', in *Early Romantics: Perspectives in British Poetry from Pope to Wordsworth*, ed. Thomas Woodman (London: Macmillan, 1998), pp. 117– 33.

[7] Beth Lau, 'Poetic Precursors (2): Spenser, Milton, Dryden, Pope', in *John Keats in Context*, ed. Michael O'Neill (Cambridge: Cambridge University Press, 2017), p. 220.

[8] Benjamin Bailey, quoted in *The Keats Circle: Letters and Papers*, ed. Hyder Edward Rollins. 2 vols. (Cambridge, MA: Harvard University Press, 1965), vol. 2, p. 269.

[9] John Keats, *Keats's Poetry and Prose*, ed. Jeffrey N. Cox (New York: Norton, 2009), p. 63, l.186.

collection with Coleridge the *Lyrical Ballads*, clearly designed as a response to Pope. Pope was the dominant figure of his generation – roughly the period of literature from 1710 to 1750 – and as such he became emblematic of Romanticism as a point of attack that could serve to differentiate the new poetics of Romanticism from what came before. And yet Bloom's *Anxiety of Influence* indicates that the forces of reaction and reception are not mutually exclusive and that even those forebears to whom a writer is most aggressive – or especially those ones – can be seen to provide blueprints for understanding the work of the subsequent generation of writers. The Romantics, it might be said, protest too much and all that protestation against Pope masks the depth of their debt to Augustan verse practices. Likewise there is every chance that the movement we call 'Augustan' might be less cohesive than we once imagined, and that the principles for which it is best known and that most clearly mark it out against Romanticism – balance, harmony, order – are not always as present as we might suppose.

This Element is an attempt to reconstruct just one of the ways in which a major aspect of Pope's poetic vision resurfaced in Romanticism by focussing on what I come to call his philosophy of appearances: how the world seems to be and how that semblance can or cannot be denoted by language. My case study for tracing the lineage of those ideas is a single work by a single mid-century poet: Mark Akenside's *Pleasure of Imagination*. I argue that Akenside is singularly instructive in uncovering the debt to subsequent poetry of Pope's approach to verse-form philosophy, even where, as in Akenside's blank verse, some of the hallmarks of Popean poetry are absent. Akenside, like many of the later Romantics, took up blank verse as a conscious movement away from the end-stopped heroic couplets that dominated the first half of the eighteenth century and that were practically synonymous with Pope. Yet many of Pope's best modern readers have found in his rhythms a far greater complexity and subtlety than stereotypes of Augustan 'balance' or 'harmony' would suggest. Pat Rogers has noted, for instance, the 'conversational' rhythms of Pope's couplets and the enormous flexibility the heroic form afforded Pope in drawing together styles and genres of poetry, even as his work accords to an Augustan mode of anti-Miltonic 'correctness'.[10] John Sitter equally works his reading of Pope's style around the principle of *decorum*, or 'the idea that different occasions call for different kinds of behavior'; thus it is more appropriate to think that 'Pope wrote in many voices' than that his metres were mechanically monotonous.[11] That plurality of voices has leant itself to a rich critical tradition of unfolding the complexities rather than the harmonious

---

[10] Pat Rogers, *Essays on Pope* (Cambridge: Cambridge University Press, 1993), p. 30.

[11] John Sitter, 'Pope's Versification and Voice', in *The Cambridge Companion to Alexander Pope*, ed. Pat Rogers (Cambridge: Cambridge University Press), pp. 37–48, p. 37.

simplicity in Pope's poetic voice over the past century.[12] It is that complexity that reopens the question of a positive influence from Augustan to Romantic poetry, and it is that which helped shape Akenside's vision of the universe and his poetic reconstruction of the world. Specifically, I argue that Pope, Akenside, and the Romantic poets are all alike concerned with appearances: with the appearance of the world, with the appearance of poetry, and finally with poetry's appearance in the world. Most recently, scholars including Tom Jones and Courtney Weiss Smith have shown that Pope's poetic language is itself complex in that it at once celebrates the artificiality of its own images and structures whilst also forming a relation with nature's images. Pope's work opens up a conversation about natural and artificial language, calling attention to poetry's own artificial character even as it appears to represent the structures of the natural world. As Weiss Smith shows, Pope's suggestion that poetry's 'Sound' can 'seem an Eccho to the Sense' is at once a natural analogy (echoes are a physical, material production) but also artificial – the semblance in play in what 'seems' to be in his poetry. In that spirit, I read semblance as a Popean product in Akenside's work and world and show how his equally complex picture of the universe – which at once affirms its own poetic artifice whilst wishing to present or represent divine nature – was Romanticism's chief debt to him. Thus through the poetic and philosophic connection of appearances, Romanticism is not at odds with all of Pope's work and thinking but is in one sense a direct successor of his ideas and working in his tradition.

It is important to stress that I am not claiming that Akenside is the only poet to take up the pressure Pope placed on appearances and artificiality and that he was thus Romanticism's only viable source for such thinking. That would be to overstate the case when what I am presenting is in fact one case study and a single telling of a story – a story told in three parts – of poetry's contribution to a discourse of appearances that was elsewhere taken for granted in Enlightenment-era philosophy. To read Akenside as a mid-century connector between Pope and Romanticism is to present one way of understanding a richer relationship between the two extreme ends of the eighteenth century and its schools of poetry than simply one of outright rejection or mythological break. *The Pleasures of Imagination* is here exemplary in that it puts into practice verse theories, literary aesthetics, and philosophical ideas in large part influenced by Alexander Pope, a poet whose name was in Akenside's day practically a byword for Neoclassical poetry. But the poem also cast its own enormous, though widely varying influence across key Romantic poets, including Wordsworth,

---

[12] See, for example, Maynard Mack, 'On Reading Pope', *College English*, vol. 7, no. 5 (1946), pp. 263–73; Howard D. Weinbrot, *Alexander Pope and the Traditions of Formal Verse Satire* (Princeton, NJ: Princeton University Press, 1982); J. Paul Hunter, 'Form As Meaning: Pope and the Ideology of the Couplet Form', *The Eighteenth Century*, vol. 37, no. 3 (1996), pp. 257–70.

Coleridge, and Keats. It participates vitally in 'the tradition of deistic verse-philosophising' that Seamus Perry has associated with Pope and Wordsworth alike and in the development of the 'creative imagination' that James Engell has charted across the long eighteenth century.[13] Crucially, it also opens up the notion of a vital overlap between the aesthetic and epistemological projects of Neoclassical and Romantic poetry. *The Pleasures of Imagination* is a complicating element that calls out the illusion in any binary understanding of those movements, highlighting deeply significant continuities that are all too easily elided by the Romantics' own myth-making. Central to my argument is the fact that *The Pleasures of Imagination* connects poets like Pope with the high Romantics in that it is a sustained attempt to 'do' philosophy in verse: it makes no attempt to dress up pre-existing ideas culled from prose-philosophical works in new clothing, but rather stages first-hand a dynamic performance of the kinds of original truths poetry can attain. These are truths that largely relate, fittingly enough, to appearances: to how the world 'appears to be' and to the nature of art and poetry themselves as special kinds of appearances in the world. This was a lesson Akenside inherited above all, as I will show, from Pope's *Essay on Man*, and in turn he provided fuel for Romantic attempts to understand man, the universe, and the fit between the two within the medium of poetry and its appearances.

Mark Akenside was born in Newcastle in 1721, a year after the final print run of Addison and Steele's popular *Spectator* newspaper and two years after Daniel Defoe's *Robinson Crusoe* and Eliza Haywood's *Love in Excess* created the market and public appetite for that most modern literary form, the novel. Akenside grew to maturity in a period when poetry, along with other artistic and cultural practices, was dominated by classical influences – what we now term the Augustan or Neoclassical period in literary history – and in which the rise of fictional and non-fictional prose forms alike forced a rethinking of the role of poetry in society. The Horatian ode enjoyed renewed popularity, poetic and critical practices were influenced by texts like Longinus's *On the Sublime*, and by far the most dominant measure in English poetry was the classically derived heroic couplet: the pairing of lines of five beats and five feet bound one to the other through the use of terminal rhymes. The most successful poet of the period bar none was Alexander Pope, whose great philosophical poem the *Essay on Man* was published between 1733 and 1734, and whose name became a byword for the meticulous metrical art of the heroic couplet. Pope is widely

---

[13] Seamus Perry, 'Wordsworth's Heroics', *The Wordsworth Circle*, vol. 34, no. 2 (2003), pp. 65–73, p. 65; James Engell, *The Creative Imagination* (Cambridge, MA: Harvard University Press, 1981).

received as the perfecter of the couplet – its greatest and most skilful proponent – and the most prominent poet of his day. He was to prove influential to the young Akenside, who (like the much later Keats) originally trained as a physician but showed yearnings towards a life of poetry from a young age; he published his *A British Philippic* in 1738 when he was aged just eighteen. Akenside published his *Pleasures of Imagination* in 1744 to immediate success and he worked and reworked the poem across the remainder of his life. An incomplete five-book version of the work under the title *The Pleasures of Imagination* appeared in 1772; though the title is only slightly changed, the poem is, as Akenside's foremost modern editor has remarked, 'very different' indeed to the earlier work.[14] With that difference in mind, except when explicitly stated, this Element is concerned with the original poem titled *The Pleasures of Imagination* – that which gained Akenside lasting fame within his lifetime, and the most often consulted by his Romantic readers. The poem itself exemplifies the mid-eighteenth-century tendency towards long blank-verse poetry with an emphasis on philosophic speculation, comparable to the earlier *Seasons* by James Thomson or to Edward Young's *Night-Thoughts* of 1742–5. It is a work of theodicy – a sustained attempt to explain and justify the world as God's creation – but also a work of natural scientific and philosophically empiricist exaction. Indeed, it is in its apparently deistic marriage of philosophical and religious perspectives that *The Pleasures of Imagination* stands alone within the landscape of eighteenth-century verse.

One of Akenside's signal achievements in the *Pleasures* was the strong pressure he exerted on individual lines of poetry and on variety as a central principle in the prosody of blank verse. It's in that sense that Akenside is a part of the long narrative in the history of verse that connects Milton and the blank-verse lines of his *Paradise Lost* with Romanticism. Generally speaking, that narrative leapfrogs over Augustan verse altogether given that Augustanism is characterized by anti-Miltonic orderly syntax and by the structuring principle of rhyme – and that presents one reason why Akenside might be thought of as an early Romantic but less as a late Augustan. Indeed, the resonances between Milton, Akenside, and Romanticism run deeper than verse form alone and Dustin D. Stewart's recent *Futures of Enlightenment Poetry* places all three figures in conversation on the topic of Enlightenment conceptions of the afterlife.[15] Yet despite that movement in verse away from Pope's couplets, this Element argues that the substance of Akenside's lines was formed in

---

[14] Dix in Mark Akenside, *The Poetical Works of Mark Akenside*, ed. Robin Dix (Cranbury, NJ: Associated University Presses, 1996), p. 18. All subsequent references to Akenside's verse and prose refer to this edition.

[15] Dustin D. Stewart, *Futures of Enlightenment Poetry* (Oxford: Oxford University Press, 2020).

response to Pope's poetics and Akenside takes up the idea of the long philosophic poem in terms that would have direct bearings on later blank-verse works like Wordsworth's *Tintern Abbey* or *The Prelude*. I argue across this Element that Akenside's debt to Pope and the Romantics' debt to Akenside can be understood in terms of a preoccupation with appearances. A major strain of Enlightenment philosophy, centred on the tradition of British empiricism, can be understood to be concerned with the way the world seems to be. The development in the seventeenth and eighteenth centuries of what we now term correspondence theories – theories of mind and world, or theories of truth that concern the balancing of mental pictures with external facts – led to highly influential models of the relation of mind to external appearances such as John Locke's *Essay Concerning Human Understanding* of 1690. (One of the best accounts of the historical development of correspondence theories of truth and Locke's role in that development, that of Richard Rorty, is also a thoroughgoing critique of such theories from the perspective of modern pragmatist philosophy.)[16] Correspondence theories also, though, led to Hume's brand of scepticism; the possible distance or difference between ideas in our minds and objects in the world left wide room for doubt and cast the reality of the world beyond our perceptions into question. It was in this culture (though prior to Humean scepticism) that Pope's *Essay on Man* addressed the world as it is experienced by men. Akenside in turn drew on Pope's *Essay* when setting into motion his own poem on the fit between mind and world, but the *Pleasures of Imagination* adapts Pope's programme by fixating on the slipperiness of appearances between what the world seems to be and what it really is. Akenside's work opens up the richness of representational knowledge, which depends upon the mind 're-presenting' images in the world and therefore offers its own direct lines of parallel with artistic making and poetic representation. Such richness and difficulties, which remain finally equivocal in Akenside, lead directly to Romanticism's own discussion of art and appearance.

This Element comprises four short sections, each designed to get at a different aspect of Akenside's unique position as a poet suspended, in history and in influence, between the mainstreams of Neoclassical verse cultures and high Romanticism in the British tradition. Each section can be read on its own terms or as part of the Element's larger argument concerning the philosophical connections and continuities of Neoclassicism and Romanticism. In that sense it broadly aims to make accessible to students, or to readers new to the questions

---

[16] See 'Mirroring' in Richard Rorty, *Philosophy and the Mirror of Nature* (Princeton, NJ: Princeton University Press, 1979), pp. 129–64.

with which this Element grapples, the major movements in poetic history between roughly the 1710s and 1810s. By focussing on those two intertwined phenomena – of appearances in the history of ideas and the role poetry played in that history – it also aims to offer a revitalized look at the period that will aid scholars who are already familiar with questions of reception and influence in the Neoclassical and Romantic period, and it extends the scholarly work done on Akenside and on his role within poetic history and tradition of the longer eighteenth century.

With this in mind, Section 1 focusses on the influence of Pope's *Essay on Man* on Akenside's poem, comparing their approaches to long philosophical poetry and their attitudes towards certainty, uncertainty, and the world of appearances. It builds on recent work on Pope to offer a brief reading of his philosophical poem the *Essay on Man*, reading it as an exemplary poem that concerns itself with the difference between how the world is and how it seems and the important consequences of that distinction for morality and for theology. Following this, Section 2 offers a reading of *The Pleasures of Imagination* on its own terms, aiming to understand the role of what Akenside calls the 'appearances in the world around us' in his poem and synthesizing that philosophical project – a project hinged upon the difficulty of identifying the difference between what *is* and what *seems to be* – with the resourcefulness of blank verse.

Section 3 departs from the *Pleasures* itself to look at its reception in the work of Samuel Taylor Coleridge, for whom Akenside's poem was a major and lasting influence in his early years as a poet. Akenside's use of terms like 'plastic' – now made all the more remarkable thanks to its treatment by Paul H. Fry in a well-known reading of William K. Wimsatt and Monroe C. Beardsley's famous article on 'The Intentional Fallacy'[17] – would be instrumental to Coleridge's own development of the 'esemplastic imagination'. Section 4 then builds on the particularities of Coleridge's reading of Akenside to consider the broader Romantic reception of the *Pleasures of Imagination*, especially in terms of its verse-form philosophizing on the nature and experience of appearances. This involves consideration of the Wordsworthian blank verse and the Keatsian 'liberal' couplet and the relation of those forms to philosophical thinking. I also argue in Section 4 that Keats's well-known notion of negative capability and its insistence on 'uncertainties' are pre-empted by what Akenside called the imagination's 'pleasures', which include a kind of joy in not knowing or remaining uncertain, as well as in knowing; as Section 1 shows, that lineage of ideas concerning uncertainty and appearances was set into motion by Pope. We broadly find, in the Romantics who were familiar with

---

[17] Paul H. Fry, *Theory of Poetry* (New Haven, CT: Yale University Press, 2012), p. 67.

Akenside's *Pleasures of Imagination*, philosophic reflections on the status of mind and world, and the fit or misfit between the two, that waver between two positions: the world as mind-dependent and the world as entirely independent of the mind. This poetics of equivocality, often understood as a hallmark of Romantic verse, constitutes the lasting legacy of Akenside's philosophical poem and its own debt to Pope.

Akenside as a figure has never been too far away from the canon of English literature, yet scholarship dealing with his work can seem surprisingly scant for all that. In recent memory, he has been championed by Robin Dix, who has done more than any other scholar to promote Akenside's work as a subject worthy of modern critical study. As well as editing a collection of essays on Akenside, Dix's major achievements include writing the invaluable *Poetical Works of Mark Akenside* and the critical biography *The Literary Career of Mark Akenside*. Before Dix, Akenside was best served by Harriet Jump, whose various essays on Akenside's writings offer new understandings of his social milieu and bring to attention previously unacknowledged manuscript versions of his poetry. Jump was also instrumental in shaping current conceptions of Coleridge's debt to Akenside in her important essay 'High Sentiments of Liberty: Coleridge's Unacknowledged Debt to Akenside'.[18] The present study of Akenside's influence on Coleridge in Section 3 is in turn indebted to Jump's work, and it also draws on seminal work by Geoffrey H. Hartman and more recent scholarship by David Vallins and Nicholas Reid.[19] In particular, Reid has influentially argued that Akenside was 'an important source for Coleridge, with his characterisation of Nature as the divine language, his exploration of models of reading and the presentation of a positive function for art as a part of that reading process, and the beginnings of the Romantic movement towards the internalisation of Christ'.[20] This Element is also indebted to Kirk M. Fabel's essay on *The Pleasures of Imagination*, which has done more than any other work to place the poem within the broader intellectual history of eighteenth-century aesthetics beyond Addison's influence.[21]

---

[18] Harriet Jump, 'High Sentiments of Liberty: Coleridge's Unacknowledged Debt to Akenside', *Studies in Romanticism*, vol. 28, no.2 (1989), pp. 207–24.

[19] Geoffrey H. Hartman, 'Reflections on the Evening Star: Akenside to Coleridge', in *New Perspectives on Coleridge and Wordsworth*, ed. Geoffrey H. Hartmann (Columbia, NY: Columbia University Press, 1972), pp. 85–131; David Vallins, 'Akenside, Coleridge, and the Pleasures of Transcendence', in *Mark Akenside: A Reassessment*, ed. Robin Dix (Cranbury, NJ: Associated University Presses, 2000), pp. 156–82; Nicholas Reid, 'Coleridge, Akenside, and the Platonic Tradition: Reading in *The Pleasures of Imagination*', *Journal of Language, Literature, and Culture*, vol. 80, no .1 (1993), pp. 31–56.

[20] Reid, 'Coleridge, Akenside, and the Platonic Tradition', p. 52.

[21] Kirk M. Fabel, 'The Location of the Aesthetic in Akenside's *Pleasures of Imagination*', *Philological Quarterly*, vol. 76, no. 1 (1997), pp. 47–68.

Akenside's poem was a literary sensation within his lifetime and, from the perspective of modern literary studies, it falls conveniently close to the mid-century; in terms of date of publication alone it offers a glimpse at verse cultures as they sat between Neoclassicism and Romanticism. This Element aims to show that what the poem can tell us about the poetry that inspired it and that it inspired is not simply what changed between Pope and the Romantics, or what was made different. Rather, it offers a uniquely instructive set of case studies in influence, continuities, and connections across the full length of the eighteenth century and beyond. These connections, as I show across the pages that follow, are thematic but also rhythmic and philosophic. Resituating Akenside at the fore of our conceptions of eighteenth-century poetry is thus invaluable when it comes to trying to understand how a phrase like 'eighteenth-century poetry' can refer equally to Pope's punishingly precise verse practices and the more fluvial movements of Wordsworth's verse and to the flexibilities of Keats's rhymes. Indeed, this Element argues that the one naturally stemmed from the other, and by turning to Akenside's verse we might begin to understand how such a lineage might be possible.

1 Philosophic Backgrounds: Pope's *Essay* and Akenside

When thinking of Akenside as a connective element poised between Neoclassical poetry and Romanticism, it is necessary in particular to begin with the poetry to which Akenside himself looked back, to which he was responding in his own verse, and from which he drew deep inspiration across his career as a poet. This opening section therefore looks to the poetry of Alexander Pope, the principal figure in poetry from shortly after the death of Dryden until the so-called Age of Johnson, from the 1710s to the 1750s and beyond, and the man widely credited with perfecting the heroic couplet. In particular I am interested in what modern readers often hail as Pope's crowning achievement, the philosophic poem the *Essay on Man* – a work that cast a long and lasting shadow across subsequent poetry, and not least the *Pleasures of Imagination*. I first reconstruct Akenside's awareness of Pope and the role Pope himself played in launching Akenside's career. I then illustrate the parallels between Pope's preface to the *Essay on Man* – a note on his philosophical intentions but also on the uses of verse in philosophizing – and Akenside's comparable preface to the *Pleasures on Man*. I then offer a brief overview and analysis of Pope's *Essay*, showing the ways in which its poetic-philosophical method were to influence Akenside. It is this understanding of Pope and of poetics that is carried forward across the rest of the Element.

When Akenside was composing *The Pleasures of Imagination*, Alexander Pope was in the latter years of his life, having dominated not just the contemporary poetry scene, but the literary scene in England more generally. In poems including *Essay on Criticism*, *The Rape of the Lock*, *Essay on Man*, and *The Dunciad*, Pope established a reputation that few poets before or since can be said to have rivalled: he was one of the earliest poets to make his living through verse alone and to live as a literary celebrity in his own lifetime; he came to embody the Neoclassical notions of wit and satire, occupying a crucial position within the network of London writers known as the Scriblerians, and he became emblematic of the verse form that would define the first half of the eighteenth century: the heroic couplet. It would not be true to say, though, that he was received with universal warmth in his own time, or that the reception of his works was free of controversy. He engaged throughout his life in public spats with other writers and publishers and was doubly suspicious as both a Catholic and a Jacobite; in his lifetime, he attracted hostile critics such as the dramatist John Dennis, who dedicated an essay to arguing that there is 'nothing more wrong, more low, or more incorrect' in poetry than Pope's *Essay on Criticism*.[22] After his death, he was relegated by Joseph Warton in his *Essay on the Genius of Pope* from a position alongside Shakespeare and Homer in the canon of English literature, and placed '*next* to *Milton*, and *just* above *Dryden*' (II. 404).[23] Subsequent generations at the beginning of the nineteenth century would use Pope's name as a touchstone for literary taste, whether they were for or against his poetic style.[24] And while it is *The Rape of the Lock* and *Essay on Man* that tend to receive the most critical attention today, Pope's bestselling works in his own time were his translations of the *Iliad* and *Odyssey*, and Warton's 1756 *Essay* proposes that 'the reputation of POPE, as a poet, among posterity, will be principally owing to his WINDSOR FOREST, his RAPE OF THE LOCK, and his ELOISA TO ABELARD'.[25] Indeed, Samuel Johnson's well-known remark on Pope's *Essay* – that 'never were of penury of knowledge and vulgarity of sentiment so happily disguised' – speaks volumes about the nature of his reception as pleasing poet foremost and thinker second, but also about the *Essay*'s divisive reception

---

[22] John Dennis, *Reflections Critical and Satyrical, Upon a Late Rhapsody Call'd, An Essay Upon Criticism* (London: B. Lintott, 1711), p. 2.

[23] Warton's *Essay* was published in two distinct parts separated by almost thirty years; Volume One appeared in 1756 and Volume Two in 1782. Joseph Warton, *Essay on the Genius and Writings of Pope*, vol. 1 (London: M. Cooper, 1756); Joseph Warton, *Essay on the Genius and Writings of Pope*, vol. 2 (London: T. Maiden, 1782).

[24] For the reception of Pope in the 1810s and 1820s, see James Chandler, 'The Pope Controversy: Romantic Poetics and the English Canon', *Critical Inquiry*, vol. 10, no. 3 (1984), pp. 481–509.

[25] Warton, *Essay*, vol. 1, p. 334.

within Pope's lifetime.[26] He was thus a poet who produced an enormous variety of verse types and forms and who also generated a broad and conflicting range of critical responses within his lifetime and beyond.

Indeed, there is a concrete link connecting Pope to Akenside's *Pleasures*, in that it may well have been because of Pope that the poem received publication in the first place. The evidence for this is only anecdotal, but the anecdotalist in question is in this case an authority: Samuel Johnson, in his brief account of Akenside in his *Lives of the Poets*, suggests that Pope read a manuscript edition of the *Pleasures* and encouraged its eventual publisher to pay generously for it. Johnson writes:

> I have heard Dodsley, by whom it was published, relate that when the copy was offered him the price demanded for it, which was an hundred and twenty pounds, being such as he was not inclined to give precipitately, he carried the work to Pope, who, having looked into it, advised him not to make a niggardly offer; for *this was no every-day writer.*[27]

If it is true then it is high praise indeed from Pope; if untrue, then it is praise from Johnson. (Notably, Dix, in retelling this anecdote, treats it as a matter of fact rather than hearsay.)[28] What it reveals is that Pope, or Johnson's Pope, from the beginning recognized the significance of Akenside's *Pleasures of Imagination*, encouraging Robert Dodsley – publisher of such works as Johnson's own *Dictionary* and Thomas Gray's *Elegy* – to invest in Akenside's future.

There is also a discernible debt to Pope in Akenside's own 'Design' to the *Pleasures of Imagination*. Though Akenside expresses a desire to stay away from the 'mock-heroic' style in his 'Design' – a term connected with Pope in the period, as it still is today, thanks to his *Rape of the Lock* and *Dunciad*[29] – his remarks on the 'turn of composition' in the poem directly connect the work to Pope's *Essay*. Akenside writes that he opted for the 'familiar epistolary of Horace' over a Virgilian poetic mode, placing himself in the Neoclassical tradition of the eighteenth century, but also, more particularly, in the tradition of the composer of many extremely popular 'Imitations of Horace'. The Horatian mode, Akenside continues, is of particular advantage as it admits 'variety of stile', an 'air of conversation', and 'closer and more concise

---

[26] I am grateful to my anonymous reader at Cambridge University Press for reminding me of Johnson's remarks and of early heated responses to Pope's *Essay* in general.

[27] Samuel Johnson, *The Works of Samuel Johnson, LL.D.*, ed. John Hawkins. 11 vols. (Cambridge: Cambridge University Press, 2011), IV. 287.

[28] Robin Dix, *The Literary Career of Mark Akenside* (Cranbury, NJ: Associated University Presses, 2006), p. 70.

[29] See Abrams's entry for 'mock epic / mock-heroic' under the heading 'Burlesque' in his *A Glossary of Literary Terms*, 6th ed. (Orlando, FL: Harcourt and Brace, 1993), p. 18.

expression'.[30] Akenside is here repeating Pope's stated primary reason for adopting verse in his *Essay*, which is for reasons of 'conciseness', from which 'the *force* as well as the *grace* of arguments' spring.[31] He continues:

> Add to this the example of the most perfect of modern poets, who has so happily applied this manner to the noblest parts of philosophy, that the public taste is in a great measure form'd to it alone.[32]

That 'most perfect of modern poets' is clearly Pope, as the context of the remark and the surrounding allusions make clear. And Akenside's remarks here make clear his appreciation of Pope and his intention to produce his own philosophic poem, but also his challenge: given that Pope has tuned the public's ear to the heroic couplet when it comes to the appreciation of verse-form philosophy, Akenside knows he will have to work to win round the reader in his comparatively relaxed blank verse.

So there are concrete reasons for thinking of Akenside as a poet in the tradition of Pope even as he moves away from the Popean couplet. Yet what concerns me here is not strong (or weak, or intermediate) evidence for Pope's having read Akenside, or for Akenside's having read Pope – though it is practically a given that Akenside did do so. Instead, I want to treat Pope as the exemplary figure of Neoclassical poetry that he is and to show that, in line with the most recent critical understandings of his work, one way of thinking of his poetic project is as a kind of philosophical meditation on appearances: the appearance of the world and the appearance of poetry in the world. It is that element of poetics that I call 'semblance', and it is semblance that, I argue across this Element, unites Pope, Akenside, and the Romantics. It is the baton of semblance that Akenside, consciously or not, picked up from Pope and his work thus stands as evidence of continuity and connection across eighteenth-century poetry. The way in which we must understand Pope's *Essay* in order to appreciate its relevance for Akenside is in its guise as a philosophic poem, one that drew on the philosophical discourses of its day. The key philosophical movement that influenced many of the long meditative poems of the eighteenth century was empiricism, and the key text in empirical philosophy was John Locke's *Essay Concerning Human Understanding*. Locke posited that we have no innate ideas and that instead all knowledge id derived from direct experience; this notion contributed to an emphasis on perception and the bodily senses in the theories of knowledge that arose over the century to follow, and it had major

---

[30] Akenside, *Poetical Works*, p. 88.

[31] Alexander Pope, *An Essay on Man*, ed. Tom Jones (Princeton, NJ: Princeton University Press, 2016), p. 4.

[32] Akenside, *Poetical Works*, p. 88.

bearings on understandings of the self in poetry too. An essential feature of Locke's thought was the division of objects of perception into their 'primary' and 'secondary' qualities: primary qualities like shape and size inhered in the objects; everything else, including taste, touch, smell, and colour, was a secondary quality. Secondary qualities of this kind are the things that individuals bring to perception of objects. As such, we might disagree about the actual shade of red that a thing is because our eyes might be subtly (or fundamentally) different in how they perceive colour; we are less likely to disagree about the size or shape of an object, thinks Locke, because those qualities exist objectively – that is, in the object. As subsequent philosophers noted – and a fact that we will find Akenside take an interest in – Locke's distinction between primary and secondary qualities highlights the possible difference between the way we see the world and the way the world really is.

By the time of English Romanticism, the detectible split between appearance and reality in philosophy had been opened up and actively pursued by Immanuel Kant, who, in his *Critique of Pure Reason*, offered a formative and influential distinction between *Schein* – mere appearance, or illusion – and *Erscheinung* – the actual appearance of the world.[33] What is crucial in Kant is that reality is nothing other than an appearance, or at least our knowledge is always limited to the way the world appears for us (what Kant calls knowledge of 'phenomena'). Thus what matters in critical philosophy is not reaching after the world 'as it really is', but rather the formulation for distinguishing with accuracy between real appearances and illusion. That was a problem or point of interest for Romanticism too, as I show in later sections of this Element, but it also existed in philosophy and in poetry before Kant developed his vocabulary of *Schein* and *Erscheinung*. George Berkeley, the second of the philosophers now known as the British empiricists, attempted to solve the problem of this difference – which we can understand as the distinction between subjective and objective reality – by claiming that all the qualities of an object are in fact what Locke called secondary qualities. Everything we see is already one of our ideas, suspended in our minds, and there is no need for what Locke called 'substance' or 'matter' to exist outside our minds in support of the qualities of objects. Berkeley's theories, known as immaterialism (the disbelief in matter) and idealism (the belief that all things exist only as ideas in our minds) were expressly designed to liberate empiricism from scepticism, but the third of the British empiricists, David Hume, would champion precisely the mode of scepticism that distinguishes between the pictures in our minds and those in the world. For Hume,

---

[33] Immanuel Kant, *Critique of the Power of Judgement*, ed. Paul Guyer (Cambridge: Cambridge University Press, 2000), p. 13.

writing against Berkeley, there was no way of achieving secure knowledge of ourselves, let alone of the world; there was, therefore, no stable basis for telling apart what we took to be real and what was really outside us. As Hume would provocatively come to phrase this idea, 'whatever *is* may *not be*'.[34]

It was in the midst of this developing set of philosophical ideas concerning the nature of appearances and their fit with reality – which twisted from certain knowledge to radical uncertainty – in which Alexander Pope wrote his *Essay on Man*. Though written between 1733 and 1734, more than a decade before Hume's *Enquiry Concerning Human Understanding*, Pope's poem responds to many of the key concerns of empiricist epistemology: the limits of human knowledge, the role of the senses and of perception in our knowledge, the relationship between mind and world, and, interwoven with the latter point, the fit between appearances in our mind and the appearances of the world. John Sitter, in a study of mid-eighteenth-century philosophical poetry, suggests that the intellectual importance of Pope's *Essay* for later poets lies in its specific adherence to a strongly empirical mode, which is to say, in its sustained meditations on perception as the source of all knowing. Sitter notes that one of Pope's apostrophes to his muse – 'Say first, of God above, of Man below / What can we reason, but from what we know?' (I. 17–18)[35] – signals Pope's 'empirical intention' as '"What we know" for Pope means primarily what we see.'[36] Indeed, one of Pope's best-known couplets from the poem appears pre-emptively to respond to Humean scepticism: 'And, spite of pride, in erring reason's spite, / One truth is clear, Whatever IS, is RIGHT' (I. 293–4). This is a deceptively simple truth claim to stir into your poem, or indeed to include as possibly the only 'clear' truth of the whole *Essay*. For Hume, what 'is' – that which 'appears' to have being – actually may not be, yet for Pope, what 'is' is right. But how so? The claim appears to be that there is little point in investigating the foundations and nature of being because what we see is what we get and what we get is therefore right. But 'rightness' implies that what exists is also in existence for the good. It suggests an optimistic morality of the Leibnizian kind, as satirized by Voltaire in *Candide*, wherein all is for the best, including the worst of the world.[37] For Tom Jones, a modern editor of Pope's poem, the phrase 'Whatever is, is right' effectively 'redescribes chance as direction: the particular unfolding of events through history in this way rather than any

---

[34] David Hume, *An Enquiry Concerning Human Understanding*, ed. Eric Steinberg (Indianapolis, IN: Hackett, 1993), XII. 3.

[35] Pope, *Essay on Man*.

[36] John E. Sitter, 'Theodicy at Midcentury: Young, Akenside, Hume', *Eighteenth-Century Studies*, vol. 12, no. 1 (1978), pp. 90–106, p. 93.

[37] Gottfried Wilhelm Leibnitz, *Essays of Theodicy on the Goodness of God, the Freedom of Man and the Origin of Evil* (Chicago, IL: Open Court, 1999).

other imaginable way will be presented as the right way, which, viewed retrospectively and as the way of getting just here, it must be'.[38] In Jones's reading, apparently contingent events are reinterpreted as, in actual fact, vital and necessary parts of God's plan, and this interpretive mode – the eye that reads reality and finds organized sense in what it reads as it goes – will directly inspire Akenside's depictions of nature as God's 'transcript' (see Section 2). Elsewhere Jones has argued that Pope's 'poetico-philosophical argument', which concerns the poem's equivocal 'defence of order, fixity and a providential scheme that nevertheless admits the force of chaos, flux and contingency', is in part enabled by Pope's revisionary practices, which admit dynamic 'changes of mind' within the static space of the page.[39] Pope also allows a major question mark to hover over his claim in the form of the weight that the word 'whatever' there carries. 'What is, is right' is different from his 'what*ever* is, is right' as the latter acknowledges the probability of a failure ever to define what it really is that *is*. Running the logic in reverse, 'what is' remains an unspecified 'whatever'. With that uncertainty acknowledged, and acknowledged within the context of one of the few ostensibly certain truths the poem will expound, the movement from 'what is' to rightness also becomes uncertain: rightness, in the sense of sound morality, receives a blow to its very foundations and begins to look shaky in spite of the couplet's confidence. At this most crucial moment in the poem, its major claim to truth, Pope is actually opening up more new questions than he answers.

This question of certainty, and the tendency of verse to keep certainty in check, is explored under the rubric of 'complexity' in some illuminating and recent critical work on Pope by Courtney Weiss Smith, who herself builds on earlier scholarship by Jones. Jones argues, in *Pope and Berkeley: The Language of Poetry and Philosophy*, that Pope's handling of poetic language equivocates between the two major understandings of language in the early eighteenth century: between natural and artificial language.[40] For Jones, Pope took seriously Berkeley's notion that nature itself is a kind of discourse – a spiritual language continuously 'spoken' by God. In that conception of the world, empiricism is a form of reading or of linguistic understanding, and the world's appearances form a kind of text. This matters because verse might therefore be seen to approximate the text of the world, by reproducing in its structures

[38] Jones in Pope, *Essay on Man*, p. xviii.

[39] Tom Jones, 'Argumentative Emphases in Pope's *An Essay on Man*', in *Voice and Context in Eighteenth-Century Verse: Order in Variety*, ed. Joanna Fowler and Allan Ingram (London: Palgrave, 2015), pp. 47–63.

[40] Tom Jones, *Pope and Berkeley: The Language of Poetry and Philosophy* (Houndmills: Palgrave, 2005), p. 1.

natural discourse. And yet, as Jones also shows, Pope was acutely aware that from a certain perspective there could be nothing less 'natural' than a poetic utterance – that the highly wrought character of verse was about as artificial as language could become. For Jones, then, the ruling tension of Pope's poetry, and the signal achievement of his poetics, is the play-off between natural and artificial accounts of language; a poem like *Essay on Man* will at once seem to want to reconstruct the universe and its great chain of being whilst at the same time drawing attention to its own fundamental differences from the world's appearances. Therefore whilst it might well seem that Pope's Augustan poetry is interested solely in order, organization, or harmony, he is very often questioning those very categories in the structures of his verse.

It is that operative word 'seems' that Weiss Smith draws attention to, and she builds on Jones's assertion that 'Pope "does not say that" sound "is an echo, a natural imitation of the sense, but only that it should seem to be so"; language thus "incorporates artifice, or seeming"'.[41] Thus Pope's well-known proposition that in poetry 'the sound must seem an eccho to the sense' is itself a 'tangle of nature and artifice', drawing together, for Weiss Smith, ideational sense and material sound in such a way that Pope 'seems to conjure and then question the dream of natural significance (which is also sometimes a dream of language's divine origin)'.[42] Weiss Smith's use of the word 'seems' – as in 'seems to conjure' – is purposeful and telling. The language, whether conceived of as reaching towards the natural or celebrating the artificial, through which Pope conducts his thinking about appearances is a rhetoric of semblance in which such ostensibly innocuous terms as 'seems' are freighted with philosophical significance. He says as much himself in the 'Design' that serves to introduce *Essay on Man*, when he suggests that his verse functions by 'steering betwixt the extremes of doctrines seemingly opposite'.[43] What appears to be an opposition may in fact be no such thing, and the 'Design' informs us that the purpose of verse – beyond its concision, as Pope writes – is its ability to open up oppositions that traditional philosophy wants to resolve or move past. This is demonstrated by Simon Jarvis in a reading of Pope's use of the notion of the 'great chain of being' in the *Essay*. Jarvis shows that a passage from the *Essay* concerning the 'great chain of being' – the notion of a hierarchically arranged universe, with God at the top and man below – is not balanced but is carried out as 'a series of little detonations of wit and rhetoric'.[44] 'These small explosions

---

[41] Courtney Weiss Smith, 'The Matter of Language; or, What Does "The *Sound* Must Seem an Eccho to the *Sense*" Mean?', *ELH*, vol. 87, no. 1 (2020), pp. 39–64, p. 42.

[42] Weiss Smith, 'The Matter of Language', p. 54.   [43] Pope, *Essay on Man*, p. 4.

[44] Simon Jarvis, 'Bedlam or Parnassus: The Verse Idea', *Metaphilosophy*, vol. 43, no. 1–2 (2012), pp. 71–81, p. 79.

leave holes in the great chain of being,' writes Jarvis. 'They leave it feeling, not like an august, divinely ordered, and unbreakable hierarchy, but, instead, like something extraordinarily vulnerable.' Jarvis's term 'august' is suggestive of the fact that this structural vulnerability would appear to be at odds with traditional accounts of Augustan verse as resolutely ordered – the kind Meyer H. Abrams, in his *Glossary of Literary Terms*, sees as essentialistic attempts to 'define' the term 'Neoclassical' against 'Romantic', as foregrounding traditionalism, an adherence to strict rules in artistic making, submission to a 'restricted position in the cosmic order', and a subsequent submission to limiting rules and conventions in poetic practice.[45] Yet it is found within one of the most influential and celebrated examples of such verse; as Weiss Smith argues, Pope's verse opens up complexity of thought and duality of meaning rather than smoothing out ideas into fixed claims. It is in this spirit that Tom Jones also applies the term 'philosophical poem' to Pope's *Essay* in a loaded sense, in that the poem does its thinking *in verse*; in Jones's terms, the poem 'instantiates a poetic philosophy, one in which necessity emerges from contingency'.[46]

Unlike the more formal philosophers of his day, Pope in his poetry opens up the possibility that 'natural' languages may not be natural at all and that the structures we find in nature – like the notion of the great chain of being explored in the *Essay on Man* – may be ones we have ourselves invented, and, as human constructs, are more fragile than they may have previously seemed. *Essay on Man* itself frequently takes up a rhetoric of semblance that complements its play of natural and artificial languages and that subtly compromises certainty of meaning, displacing claims about 'what is' with mere appearances. To say, as Pope does, that 'Death still draws nearer, never seeming near' (III. 76), is to say that appearances belie the awful reality of mortal being. When writing of the causal force that lies behind human passion in Book II of the *Essay*, Pope suggests that it is 'real good, or seeming, moves them all' (II. 94). That casual invocation of appearances entirely alters the character of the claim being made, though it is notably unclear what the judgement of semblance applies to: it might be that it only *seems* to be the case that passions are moved by the 'real good' in nature. Or, more troubling, it might be that the goodness that seems 'real' to us is only so in appearance – that even the things that seem good to us might in fact not be so. That would be the polar opposite of rightness being 'what is', and here there is the suggestion that what seems right or good is in fact not.

That rhetoric carries over into the theological speculations of the poem, in which the world's spiritual status is largely a question of how it appears to us (as

---

[45] Abrams, *Glossary of Literary Terms*, pp. 125–7.   [46] Jones in Pope, *Essay on Man*, p. xviii.

when doubt is explored as an empirical activity, when 'sacred seem'd th'etherial vault no more' [III.263]). Very often the poem presents us with ambiguities built into the language of semblance itself, as in the following couplet:

> What crops of wit and honesty appear
> From spleen, from obstinacy, hate, or fear! (II. 185–6)

That use of the verb 'appear' would present itself as a synonym of something like the phrase 'arise from': wits and honesty arise, somewhat paradoxically, from negative qualities such as spleen or hate. But we are also permitted to see this as only an appearance – that those virtues only *seem* to stem from negative qualities and in fact might be entirely divorced from them if we probe a little further. The same ambiguity is woven into the central tension of the poem by lines in Book I: 'Better for Us, perhaps, it might appear / Were there all harmony, all virtue here' (I. 165). At this stage of the poem Pope is entertaining the notion of a world in which that most Augustan of principles, harmony, was pushed to its furthest extent. Perhaps it would be better if 'never air or ocean felt the wind; / That never passion discompos'd the mind' – and that play on composition will remind us of the ideal of perfectly harmonic verse. The images Pope gives us are strangely barren ones, however: in a poem in which God's presence can be felt on the breeze (the natural language of the 'whispering Zephyr' in line 205 of Book I, for instance), an ocean untroubled by the wind seems not just materially static but spiritually bereft. And the comparison is immediately made to the human mind: what of a mind untroubled by its passions, of, perhaps, reason perfected? Pope tells us that 'ALL subsists by elemental strife / And Passions are the elements of Life'. So there is a 'gen'ral ORDER', but the operative word there is 'general'. Strife is not just permitted in nature; it is the condition of passion and figures as, amongst other things, the source of religious knowledge. Crucially, this verse paragraph is all hinged upon semblance and upon the fact that 'it might appear' better for us if harmony were an absolute and ruling principle in the world and in verse alike. As Pope's poem will repeatedly strive to prove, appearances can and will deceive us.

Pope effectively doubles down on that particular instance of the slipperiness of appearances only a handful of lines later, in the next verse paragraph. Returning to a dominant theme of the poem, man's presumption to know beyond his own station, he notes that man 'appears' just as 'griev'd when looking downwards to animal life as when he looks upwards towards angels (I. 175–6). That is because man envies the qualities of animals that he does not have: the strength of the bull or the fur of the bear. The lesson here is that God has distributed amongst creation the 'proper organs' to the appropriate creatures, and man, 'whom rational we call' (I. 187), should recognize his own privileged position as the only reasoning creature rather than focus on what he lacks. There is thus a probable pun in what Pope calls the 'seeming want' of man (I. 181). It is at once an ostensible but not actual deficit – 'want' as 'lack' – but it is also 'want' as 'desire' and the want for seemingness or semblance. A 'seeming want' in the context of the broader discussions of empiricism and appearances in *Essay on Man* figures as the desire, not to be fulfilled, of a kind of authenticity or reliability of appearances where truth and perception coincide. The lesson of the poem is, in many respects, to acknowledge that such an absolute form of truth is not attainable, at least not to man.

Pope, then, very clearly develops a different approach to truth than the philosophical writings of Locke or the mathematics of Newton, Pope's forebears. Harry M. Solomon accordingly writes against those who approach the *Essay* 'as either philosophy or poetry but not as the kind of text it was and is: a philosophical poem ... neither the logocentric discourse of traditional philosophy and history of ideas nor the aesthetic discourse of traditional literary history and literary criticism suffices'.[47] This would put it at odds with a label often attached to the *Essay* and to Akenside's poem: that of didactic poetry. Didacticism implies pre-existing truths that are bundled in verse as communicable content. Instead, as Maynard Mack writes, for Pope, poetry is 'not history, but a form of action within history that has a history'; it is 'a configuration of elements arranged in dramatic and dynamic poise by an entirely human wit' and not a static presentation (or re-presentation) of truths.[48] In truth, both Pope and Akenside can be thought of as producing a variety of didactic verse; both poets wrote prose 'Argument' sketches ahead of the Books of their poems and both expressed a desire to instruct as well as to entertain in the sketches of the 'Design' of each poem. Yet they are not simply didactic in the sense that they wish to present facts in verse, but rather the poems want to engage the reader with thoughts in process. Indeed, Pope's verses constantly unstitch or undermine themselves, or else pull in two directions at once – his truths are equivocal and he generates a far more complex and fragile picture of the universe than one of simple order under God.

As Kirk Fabel has influentially argued, the manner of reading 'philosophical poetry' established by Harry Solomon is useful for considering Akenside as one of Pope's successors, and it is in this area that critical revaluation of Akenside's work – which is still ongoing in light of the landmark scholarship of Robin Dix – is thrown most starkly into relief.

---

[47] Harry M. Solomon, *The Rape of the Text: Reading and Misreading Pope's* Essay on Man (Tuscaloosa: University of Alabama Press, 1993), p. 183.

[48] Maynard Mack, ed., *The Last and Greatest Art: Some Unpublished Poetical Manuscripts of Alexander Pope* (Newark: University of Delaware Press, 1984), p. 16.

Akenside's own philosophical poetry, as Fabel writes, 'achieves a density through its alternating depictions of aesthetic experience'.[49] A decade and a half prior, Robert D. Stock had described that same philosophical poetry as marked by an 'indistinctness, or perhaps one should say, elusiveness, of thought', to such an extent that 'the modern reader is apt to find it as unappealing'.[50] At least within the current critical field of historical poetics, modern sensitive readers are apt to appreciate the ways in which a certain indistinctness of thought can be understood as a continuation of the thinking that wants to steer betwixt opposing doctrines of thought, and Akenside, like Pope, can be understood as wanting to resist crystallizing ideas into a currency for doctrine or dogma. Akenside, like Pope, resists easy assimilation into the simple form of didactic poetry precisely because he performs, rather than represents, truth and knowledge; as Megan Kitching writes, 'Philosophical poetry in its more didactic guise seems to lack the imaginative dimensions or emotional appeal of, say, the blank verse meditations of Mark Akenside, Edward Young or William Wordsworth.'[51]

Let us return, in closing, to Pope's apparent maxim that 'whatever is, is right'. As I have suggested, much of the difficulty of that notion stems from the fact that there's no obvious way of discerning what really 'is'. In that respect there's an intrinsic tension in two of the poem's concluding maxims:

> For Wit's false mirror held up Nature's light;
> Shew'd erring Pride, WHATEVER IS, IS RIGHT;
> That REASON, PASSION, answer one great aim;
> That true SELF-LOVE and SOCIAL are the same;
> That VIRTUE only makes our Bliss below;
> And all our Knowledge is, OURSELVES TO KNOW.
>
> *(IV. 398)*

By now the poem has established well the notion that man's knowledge should be of man, or at least of human concerns and not God. And it has made the case for that notion by demonstrating that the sources of human knowledge – the senses – cannot penetrate beyond physical matters into metaphysical ones. Yet given that our senses are limited in scope and cannot see the world in all its glory, how can it be argued that 'whatever is, is right'? Or, more to the point, we might ask what good is such an argument: it may well be true that *whatever* is, is

---

[49] Fabel, 'Location of the Aesthetic', p. 54.

[50] Robert D. Stock, *The Holy and the Daemonic from Sir Thomas Browne to William Blake* (Princeton, NJ: Princeton University Press, 1982), p. 169.

[51] Megan Kitching, '"When Universal Nature I Survey": Philosophical Poetry before 1750', in *Voice and Context in Eighteenth-Century Verse: Order in Variety*, ed. Joanna Fowler and Allan Ingram (London: Palgrave, 2015), pp. 83–100, p. 83.

right, but, given that we cannot move past semblance, we are destined never to know what rightness really is. The moral lesson of the poem remains out of reach and instead we get only appearances like the poem itself – a 'false mirror held up [to] Nature's light'. The question of appearances in relation to that line is inescapable, and in its appearance early in Book IV, this time safely contained in scare quotes, Jones adds, in his editor's notes, the telling observation that here the phrase implies 'an acceptance of circumstances that do not initially seem optimal' (85). Indeed, even after things have begun to 'seem optimal' to Pope, his poem makes clear that they will only ever *seem* one way or the other – it is an exercise in the reading of appearances rather than an inquiry into the actual nature of being.

Pope's poem is, then, a philosophic poem in a thoroughgoing sense, but its philosophy is concerned with questions that traditionally belong to the category of aesthetics rather than ontology. We are not going to be able to get at the way things are in order to judge what is right, but we should be attending instead to that which we can apprehend: the appearance of reality. As Jones has shown, natural reality, for Pope, does indeed appear structured, but the structure of his own verses calls into question the validity of that appearance. His poetry constantly grapples with natural verses and artificial structures without resolving the two, giving us alternating appearances of each as more superior, or more closer to truth, or more spiritually significant. As an idea, that shifting play of appearances would seem in itself to take us quite far from the mainstream ideals of Augustan poetry – and yet Pope is the exemplar of that tradition, destabilizing its categories of 'harmony' and 'order' at the same time as he establishes them. It is that subtler form of Augustan poetics and that counter narrative to simple order in poetry that Akenside found in Pope. In the 'Design' to the *Pleasures*, he begins with the claim that 'there are certain powers in human nature which seem to hold a middle place between the organs of bodily sense and the faculties of moral perception'. That is a very clear echo of Pope's suggestion that his verses would navigate 'betwixt' extremities of thought. But it also takes up the rhetoric of semblance, to point to the role appearances – mere appearances, or the actual and vital appearances of the natural and spiritual world – play in our comprehension of reality. *Essay on Man* sets the template for rethinking Enlightenment-period debates about knowledge and perception by focussing on the aesthetic question at the centre of those epistemological and ontological debates: the question of appearances. And in the *Pleasures of Imagination* and on to the mainstream of Romantic poetry we will see poets draw on that template to think about art's own capacity for mirroring the universe, or for forming its own kind of appearance in the world.

2 'Appearances in the World around Us': Akenside and the Way Things Seem to Be

In an essay that argues for Akenside's use of 'Evening-Star' imagery as conceptually distinct from similar images in the Romantics, the great critic of the long eighteenth century Geoffrey Hartman observes that 'in the Romantic poets the nature lyric is as much about consciousness as about nature'.[52] Thanks in large part to Hartman's own career as a Romanticist, along with seminal critical works of the twentieth century including Abrams's *Correspondent Breeze* and the essays edited by Harold Bloom in *Romanticism and Consciousness*, such a view of Romantic nature poetics has stuck, and it is indeed now all but a truism that the Romantic world acts as a mirror of the subject's mind.[53] Yet, in restating the truism that Romantic nature reflects human consciousness within the context of a discussion of Akenside, Hartman aims at sharpening a further distinction: between eighteenth-century depictions of nature in verse and those of Romanticism. This is to overlook the fact that Akenside's signal achievement, his *Pleasures of Imagination*, is deeply involved with the workings of consciousness in the face of encounters with nature. John Norton – in an essay that was notably published the same year Hartman originally delivered his theses on Akenside and the Romantics – goes so far as to claim that the poem 'is not about the natural world' at all, but rather it 'concerns the processes involved when the mind confronts the natural world or its representation in some artistic medium'.[54] There is some provocation in Norton's claim that the poem isn't really concerned with nature '*at all*', but unorthodox as it seems, his view has proven influential. Subsequent criticism has done much to reinstate a sense of the perceiving and thinking subject in understandings of Akenside's poem. Yet it is still worth appreciating that, in the same year, two critics could read the same work so differently: as a poem concerned with nature in itself, separate from the mind; and as a poem barely about nature at all, but instead entirely about the beholding mind. It is striking indeed that the same text can appear so different to different eyes.

This section is an attempt to make sense of these divergent ways of reading *Pleasures of Imagination* – as about nature or as about consciousness, and as a late flourishing of the Augustan style or as a proto-Romantic text – by understanding it precisely as a poem obsessed with the strangenesses of

---

[52] Hartman, 'Reflections on the Evening Star', p. 86.

[53] See Geoffrey H. Hartman, *Wordsworth's Poetry, 1787–1814* (New Haven, CT: Yale University Press, 1964); Meyer H. Abrams, *The Correspondent Breeze* (New York: Norton, 1984); Harold Bloom, ed., *Romanticism and Consciousness* (New York: Norton, 1970).

[54] John Norton, 'Akenside's *The Pleasures of Imagination*: An Exercise in Poetics', *Eighteenth-Century Studies*, vol. 3, no. 3 (1970), pp. 366–83, p. 369.

appearances: of how the world appears to us, how it appears for us, how it seems to be, and how it really is. Built into the language of appearances and semblance in *Pleasures of Imagination* is a very real sense that the way the world seems to be may very well not be how it is at all. Understanding it in this light places it in the tradition of Pope's *Essay on Man* and the philosophical-poetic exploration of how the world seems to be; Akenside's thinking, like Pope's, is largely dependent on the structures of his verse. This present section also lays the foundations for thinking through Akenside's major influence on the Romantic poets and thus on his role as a hinge between Neoclassical and Romantic verse philosophy.

To get at the philosophical aspect of Akenside's verse the poem need not be 'translated into more meaningful terminology' as Norton contends, in a reading of *Pleasures of Imagination* that understands elements of Akenside's text strictly as restatements of Lockean or other philosophic doctrines.[55] Indeed, as this section makes clear, it is precisely the singularity of poetic expression, coupled with the unique capabilities of verse that lets Akenside sing apart from a figure like Locke. In a sense, to read Akenside otherwise is to read against the argument of *Pleasures of Imagination* itself. Book II begins, as Akenside glosses it in his prose 'Argument', by meditating on 'the separation of imagination from philosophy' in then current writers and the possibility of their reunion in verse form.[56] Early on in that book Akenside writes that 'Arm'd with the lyre, already have we dar'd / To pierce divine philosophy's retreats, / And teach the Muse her lore' (II. 62–4). Poetry here is a weapon, philosophy a kind of physical space or set of spaces to be invaded. Yet what Akenside actually seeks is the fusion of, in his words, 'truth and beauty', with the kinds of 'deep argument' he 'sang' in Book I (II. 66–7). Thus poetical phrasing should not, in his own estimation, be paraphrased in order to understand its truths – the truths are sung. Norton continues by saying that 'one of the major problems in criticizing *The Pleasures of Imagination* is that its diction is highly figurative and does not always lend itself to clarity or explicitness'.[57] But rather than try to will ourselves past what is unclear or not explicit in a poem, we as critics may do well to respect those difficulties: to ask whence and how they arise and to reflect on the kinds of thinking they demand of us in place of furnishing us with answers. What is it about *Pleasures of Imagination* that resists simple restatement or prose 'translation', and how does this stubborn complexity feed into a kind of philosophic mode and a kind of thinking in verse? These

---

[55] Norton, 'Akenside's *The Pleasures of Imagination*', p. 370.

[56] Akenside, *Poetical Works*, p. 110.

[57] Norton, 'Akenside's *The Pleasures of Imagination*', p. 377.

are the questions this section attempts to work through by offering a new reading of *Pleasures of Imagination* with appearances in mind.

There is an indisputable debt at work in *Pleasures of Imagination* to Joseph Addison's essays on the 'Pleasures of the Imagination', published in 1712 across issues 411 to 422 of his periodical *The Spectator*. The title of Akenside's poem is the giveaway, but he also alludes to Addison's influential essays in his prose 'Design' to the poem. Indeed, criticism has been at pains to express the full extent of Akenside's borrowings from Addison.[58] Yet the relationship between prose-form philosophic essays and verse-form long poem are far from straightforward, as criticism has also noted. Steve Clark, for instance, has done much, to show that Addison's Locke is not the same as Akenside's Locke and that *Pleasures* reveals an original reading of *Essay Concerning Human Understanding* that focusses on the active or 'lab'ring' mind.[59] In this sense, as with the better-known case of Pope's use of Bolingbroke's ideas in *Essay on Man*, the two 'Pleasures of Imagination' offer an instructive case study in conceptions of the different philosophic workings of prose and verse forms in the period. For all the similarities in their models of imagination and their debt to Lockean empiricism, they stand alone as different texts in almost everything but title and topic.

All the same, Addison's essay is vitally important for understanding the background of one area of Akenside's poem and its thinking: the slippery relationship between perceiving mind and perceived world and the possible distinctions between reality and appearance. Addison's essays, as noted, are steeped throughout in Lockean philosophy, and the debt to the tenets of empiricism in both Addison and Akenside are large.[60] In particular, Addison in his criticism is attuned to the theory of truth underpinning Locke's account of knowledge – of the need for ideas in our minds to 'fit' with objects in the world – and he exploits many of the deeper consequences of this thinking in his essays. He paraphrases Locke as follows: 'Light and Colours, as apprehended by the Imagination, are only Ideas in the Mind, and not Qualities that have any Existence in Matter.'[61] Consequent to this fact, writes Addison, 'we are every where entertained with pleasing Shows and

---

[58] On this topic, see Robert Marsh, 'Akenside and Addison: The Problem of Ideational Debt', *Modern Philology*, vol. 59, no. 1 (1961), pp. 36–48; and John L. Mahoney, 'Addison and Akenside: The Impact of Psychological Criticism on Early English Romantic Poetry', *The British Journal of Aesthetics*, vol. 6, no. 4 (1966), pp. 365–74.

[59] Steve Clark, '"To Bless the Lab'ring Mind": Akenside's *The Pleasures of Imagination*', in *Mark Akenside: A Reassessment*, ed. Robin Dix (London: Associated University Presses, 2000), pp. 132–52.

[60] See Marsh, 'Akenside and Addison'.

[61] Addison, Joseph and Richard Steele, eds., *The Spectator*, 413 (24 June 1712).

Apparitions' in which 'our souls are at present delightfully lost and bewildered in a pleasing Delusion, and we walk about like the Enchanted Hero of a Romance, who sees beautiful Castles, Woods and Meadows; and at the same time hears the warbling of Birds, and the purling of Streams'. This is surely strange: a large part of the 'pleasure' of Addison's title refers to the fact that the images our minds receive and that thus furnish the 'imagination' are involved in 'pleasing Delusion'. What, we might ask, is so pleasurable about being deceived by our senses or of the constant risk of such deception? Addison's immediate attempt to account for this pleasure rests on a literary analogy: we are like figures in a medieval Romance, seeing and hearing things that will turn out to be unreal; for, as Addison continues, 'upon the finishing of some secret Spell, the fantastic Scene breaks up, and the disconsolate Knight finds himself on a barren Heath, or in a solitary Desart'.[62] Addison's 'pleasure' here is the delusion brought about by the images in our mind interacting with those of the senses. These are Locke's two categories of ideas – those formed of past perceptions, housed in our minds as experience, and those immediately and ineluctably drawn in by the senses. In epistemological terms, we should be able to detect with ease the differences between the two, at least if we want to maintain a coherent notion of truth in an objective sense. But in Addison's essays on aesthetics, a key part of the pleasure derived from the imagination consists in the confusion of ideas in the mind and the experience of the world, and in the muddying of appearances and reality. This leads Addison into deep reflection on the nature of art and representation. Mimetic art copies nature's appearances and, in its status as a kind of pleasurable delusion, it communicates something of the slipperiness of appearances we see in the world around us. In this sense, art's 'truth' can be said to rest in its status as fabrication.

That appearances can either be real or delusional ('mere' appearances) is contained neatly in the word 'semblance', a key term in aesthetics and epistemology of the eighteenth century which is nevertheless markedly equivocal despite its important role in philosophy. Semblance describes the way the world seems to be, though the way something 'seems to be' can at once signal a truth about that thing or else what that thing *is not*. What Addison means by 'truth' in the Lockean sense is thus the agreement between appearances and reality – where the pictures in our minds accord with facts in the world and do not form delusions. Modern philosophy calls this a 'correspondence theory' of truth, where what is true depends upon just

---

[62] For commentary on this moment in Addison, see Dustin D. Stewart, 'Akenside's Refusal of Allegory: *The Pleasures of Imagination* (1744)', *Journal for Eighteenth-Century Studies*, vol. 34, no. 3 (2011), pp. 315–33, p. 318.

such a correspondence between mind and world, and it was the dominant theory of the nature of truth in eighteenth-century philosophy, thanks largely to Descartes' and Locke's pictures of the mind. This matters because Akenside, in his own attempt to think through the 'Pleasures of the imagination', is clearly concerned with correspondence and with the world as appearance. He begins Book III of the poem with a prolonged meditation on the nature of truth, in terms of knowledge and also of morality:

> where the pow'rs
> Of fancy neither lessen nor enlarge
> The images of things, but paint in all
> Their genuine hues, the features which they wore
> In nature; there opinion will be true,
> And action right.
>
> *(III. 18–23)*

Where the images we hold in our minds are correctly aligned with the appearances of things in the world, therein lies truth. It is on such truths that morality (or 'action right' – a decidedly Popean way of speaking) depends. Taken in one sense, the beginning of Book III serves as a warning about what is at stake in mental representation, one that paves the way for the subsequent discussion of the powers and role of poetry in Book III, and Akenside will state quite clearly that art's images cannot outdo those of nature:

> For not th' expanse
> Of living lakes in summer's noontime calm,
> Reflects the bord'ring shade and sun-bright heav'ns
> With fairer semblance.
>
> *(III.358–61)*

Art cannot be better than nature, but it risks being worse than it; reflecting is not the same as reality. Yet the 'semblance' that is the artwork carries the potential of pleasurable delusion. As for Addison, one of the key pleasures of the imagination lies as much in delusion as it does in truth. This is the strangeness, then, of the discussion of appearances in Book III: that truth lies in the stable relationship between image and thing, but appearances in our minds – and, to a stronger degree still, appearances in artworks and poems – are very often not stable at all. This notion will colour the poem in general.

Akenside opens the prose 'Design' to *Pleasures of Imagination* by invoking precisely this sense of semblance. 'There are', he writes, 'certain powers in human nature which seem to hold a middle place between the organs of bodily sense and the faculties of moral perception: They have been call'd by a very

general name, THE POWERS OF IMAGINATION'.[63] Describing the imagination as an intermediary between mental moral activity and the body's senses, it
is by no accident that Akenside also invokes the in-betweenness of semblance to
describe that intermediary position: they '*seem* to hold' a middle place. Indeed,
the entire 'Design', as well as setting up the relationship between the titular
'pleasures' of imagination and 'the agreeable appearances of nature',[64] also sets
up a sense of the difficulties in distinguishing between appearances and reality,
and this sense of complexity is only compounded when we come to consider the
role of art and poetry in reproducing the world. Given that the world already
meets us as appearance – where 'appearance' can be either actual or illusory –
the poetic artwork, as its own kind of appearance (what we saw Akenside call
poetry's 'semblance'), adds a further layer of complexity. Akenside is quite
clear on this, writing of the 'Particular pleasure' of 'that various and complicated resemblance existing between several parts of the material and immaterial
world which is the foundation of metaphor and wit'.[65] Ideas and objects
resemble one another, but they do so in a complicated and non-
straightforward way; it is this complexity of relations that opens up room for
Addison's 'delightful' delusion. Material and immaterial parts do fit, in an
analogous relationship to one another, yet the fit is loose to the extent that
there is a frisson or pleasure found in their uncertain relations. Such uncertainty
of thinking is central to the aesthetics of the long philosophic poem as Akenside
developed it and as Romanticism received it, and it was a ruling concern, as
shown in the previous section, of Pope's poetic plays on appearances. Akenside,
then, is an inheritor of a tradition, established by Pope, of reflecting but also
challenging Enlightenment philosophy within verse.

Akenside's statements on poetic form (glossed by him as 'stile') are also
framed around the central theme of appearances, and it is here that Akenside's
philosophy is seen to develop in step with his verse practices. This is at once to
oppose any overly hasty understanding of his work in accordance with a 'form/
content' divide – where verse is mere ornament for philosophic ideas – and also
to bring Akenside in line with understandings of verse practices more often
discussed in relation to Romantic poetry. Akenside acknowledges that, because
he is working with 'whatever our imagination feels from the agreeable appearances of nature', a more fluvial structure than rhyming couplets also 'appear'd
more natural' to him.[66] As he puts it, 'the subject before us tending almost
constantly to admiration and enthusiasm, seem'd rather to demand a more open,
pathetic and figur'd stile'.[67] Crucially, at this moment Akenside once again

---

[63] Akenside, *Poetical Works*, p. 85.   [64] Akenside, *Poetical Works*, p. 86.
[65] Akenside, *Poetical Works*, p. 87.   [66] Akenside, *Poetical Works*, pp. 86, 88.
[67] Akenside, *Poetical Works*, p. 88.

asserts the way things 'seem to be' in the process of artistic making. By the close of the 'Design', and by the time he is reflecting on his own methods and principles of composition, Akenside has insensibly transitioned from writing about nature's appearances to the appearance of his own poem, a movement that charts the development of his philosophical thinking into a poetical style. It is this sense of the artwork as a kind of constructed 'appearance', and as one that deals with natural appearances or 'semblances', that is at stake in *Pleasures of Imagination*.

Early on in the first book of the poem, Akenside affirms that 'not alike to every mortal eye / Is this great scene unveil'd' (I. 79–80). He will repeat such proto-Romantic statements, on the subjective nature of perception, in lines from Book III that deal with poetic composition: 'the course / Of things external acts in different ways / On human apprehensions' (III. 14–16). There is an element here of Blake's later statements on the subject of subject-ive perception, such as 'the Fool sees not the same tree as the wise man' in *Marriage of Heaven and Hell*.[68] For Akenside, there is a logic in play here that is difficult to separate into causes and effects: it is the 'claims / Of social life' that bracket men into different modes of seeing; as Vallins glosses this passage, Akenside has in mind scientific materialists, the immaterialist specu-lations of the philosophers, and the visionary loftiness of poets.[69] This would indicate that different vocations or stations in life enable or encourage us to see nature differently. In fact we appear to have those vocations thrust upon us by nature itself: 'with wise intent / The hand of nature on peculiar minds / Imprints a diff'rent byass, And to each / Decrees its province in the common toil' (I. 82–5). We are, in fact, worked on differently by nature's impressions, and so are in turn made fit for different forms of work. 'Bias' is an odd word to choose for this process, implying as it does prejudice or pre-judgment: the thinking we do prior to experience. The 'peculiarity' of these minds is here emphasized, suggesting that, though nature is the causal agent here, it works with the material it is given and makes of us what it can. This matters because a notion like 'poetic genius', or 'genius', or simply an exalted figure of the 'poetic' type, depends on some 'natural' state of mind prior to experience. Akenside's passage equivocates, deferring between internal and external sources for his higher minds – those individuals to whom 'the sire omnipotent unfolds / The world's harmonious volume' (more on this concept will follow in Section 3). A question therefore remains tantalizingly unanswered: Are such minds elect and plucked out by divinity from the moments of their births?

---

[68] Blake, *Complete Poetry & Prose of William Blake*, p. 35.
[69] Vallins, 'Akenside, Coleridge, and the Pleasures of Transcendence', p. 157.

Or are they rather the products of individual natural educations to be charted as the growth of the poet's mind?

Those questions matter because they make it difficult to speak of anything like the work's political bent, even as the poem informs us that mankind is divided – somehow, in some way – into social strata. It gives us a Popean notion of hierarchy, complete with the indication that 'whatever IS, is RIGHT', but it does not tell us if those perceived classes are fixed and rigid or if they can be worked around and ascended. To an extent, though, the reactions we have to natural forms will indicate something of our worth in the eyes of divinity, and so Akenside wants to convince us that cultivating personal taste and training ourselves to experience pleasure – the pleasures of the imagination as it scans the 'world's harmonious volume' – will enable us to understand our own place within the intricately structured system of the universe. Reading God's work, then, is an activity that accords with the blueprints of *Essay on Man* and its ruling directive: 'Know then thyself' (II. 2). The poet is ordained 'Thro' life and death to dart his piercing eye / With thoughts beyond the limit of the frame' (I. 156–7), and in this way Akenside encourages us to develop taste in ourselves as readers: to think beyond the 'frame' of the work of art, or the limits of the poem's page, and to construct meaning for ourselves using the images at hand as a starting point. This is a notably subjectivist approach to truth, one that flies in the face of simple correspondence theories such as that expounded by Locke.

What Akenside tells us is that, though we are encountering objects when we encounter nature, by virtue of our own statuses as self-conscious beings, the way in which we encounter those objects is subjective. Realizing this will help us understand the nature of the pleasures, described by Akenside in his poem, which are to be derived from nature and taken up by the imagination. To experience nature in an explicitly 'subjective' way is, as Norton argues, at the same time to experience the self: nature becomes a kind of mirror in which we catch flashes of our own minds working. This is indeed fairly explicit within the poem, as is made clear in lines from Book III:

> O! teach me to reveal the grateful charm
> That searchless nature o'er the sense of man
> Diffuses, to behold, in lifeless things,
> The inexpressive semblance of himself,
> Of thought and passion.
>
> *(III. 279–86)*

The poet is asking the power in nature to help him reveal the charm that nature itself 'diffuses' over man and that allows man to see in the object world 'the inexpressive semblance' of himself. 'Semblance' matters here, as 'resemblance' would be untenable not only in terms of the line's rhythm – rather, where 'resemblance' implies a simple likeness or similitude, 'semblance' holds together similitude with a more profound sense of visionary appearance, and of the appearance of man unto man. Never mind that this is an 'inexpressive' semblance, one that shows no emotion, or perhaps, in the context of poetic expression, one that bespeaks or yields no truth. There are further complications in play here: lifeless things, for one, throw out only inexpressive semblances, but is man's sense of himself then also without life? The wording here also presents the ambiguities that can arise without a clarifying Oxford comma. Is the semblance of man to be equated to the contents of that auxiliary clause (man's semblance consists of natural thought and passion), or are those instead separate items on the list (there is man's semblance, then there is thought, then there is passion)? Whether or not we read this as a list-form sequence or as two descriptions of the same image will govern whether we see in these lines mere solipsism – man looks at nature and sees only man – or a glimpse of the deeper power of a thinking, feeling force operating through the lifeless forms of the world.

In short, these brief lines are anything but straightforward and they take us to the central ambiguities of appearances in *Pleasures of Imagination*. The poem repeatedly plays with the notion of truth it puts forward – that truth equals the balancing of images in the mind with facts in the world – by showing the ways in which the imagination itself tends towards delightful misapprehension. One way in which the imagination can enter into a pleasing delusion is to imagine the world as it exists when we are not looking at it, or, in the same vein, to imagine those parts or aspects of the universe that no man can ever see. Peter Knox-Shaw, in a brief note on *Pleasures of Imagination*, draws attention to this aspect of the poem's thinking, highlighting what he calls the image of 'unseen stars' in Book I:[70]

> Now amaz'd she views
> Th'empyreal waste, where happy spirits hold
> Beyond this concave heav'n, their calm abode;
> And fields of radiance, whose unfading light
> Has travell'd the profound six thousand years,
> Nor yet arrives in sight of mortal things.
>
> *(I: 201–6)*

Here Akenside gives the reader an impossible view: starlight that, having travelled for six thousand years, has yet to reach the 'sight of mortal things'. The phrasing here is tight and precise and, rather than suggesting light that 'has

---

[70] Peter Knox-Shaw, 'Unseen Stars: Addison, Akenside, Young, and Huygens', *ANQ*, vol. 32, no. 4 (2019), pp. 227–30. p. 227.

not reached earth' or something similar, Akenside quite specifically invokes human perception of such light, thus emphasizing the impossibility of the sight unseen. 'Sight' in line 206 forms a natural pairing with 'light' in 204 – what Hugh Kenner would call, in the context of Pope's Augustan poetics, a perfectly 'reasonable rhyme'[71] – but no such easy correspondence is in fact permitted in this unrhymed poem. What we are given is the kind of view that is well known as a hallmark of Romantic poetics, exemplified by Shelley's image, in *Mont Blanc*, of the 'solitary' and 'silent' snows and winds that no human can see or hear at the top of the mountain, leading to the question: 'And what were thou, and earth, and stars, and sea, / If to the human mind's imaginings / Silence and solitude were vacancy?'.[72] Those 'imaginings' are of central concern, as Shelley, like his Romantic peers, took the imagination to be the mind's ability to peer beyond the limits of perception, or at least the faculty that can try to do so; to this extent, the presentation of an unseeable sight is a literary poetic device developed by Akenside and counted as one of the 'pleasures of imagination' – the point where the mind stops passively receiving sights and information from the universe, and enters into an active gear to generate for itself new meanings and new images beyond what it has already experienced.

The imagination can present to us (often pleasantly) images that we could not possibly see, but it can also form connections in our minds beyond those that we can possibly experience in the world. A central dynamic of *Pleasures of Imagination* is the intersecting nature of material and immaterial substances, and the possibility of imagining how spirit operates in and through solid objects. Again in Book III Akenside writes:

> Such are the various aspects of the mind –
> Some heav'nly genius, whose unclouded thoughts
> Attain that secret harmony which blends
> Th'æthereal spirit with its mold of clay.
>
> *(III. 278–81)*

The mind has some kind of access to the secret connection between ether-like spirit and the solid substances of reality, here represented by the clay from which the first man was formed. This connection is 'secret' because it is not empirically knowable – it cannot be seen or experienced first-hand. Our imaginations can nevertheless gain a sense of how such things come to be connected by reflecting on its own operations: because the imagination is the faculty that synthesizes and connects very different things (enabling amongst other things,

---

[71] Hugh Kenner, 'Pope's Reasonable Rhymes', *ELH*, vol. 41, no. 1 (1974), pp. 74–88.

[72] Percy Bysshe Shelley, *Shelley's Poetry and Prose*, ed. Donald H. Reiman and Neil Freistat (New York: Norton, 2002), 48, ll.142–4.

as Akenside writes, the poetic art of metaphor), turning sustained attention to the workings of the imagination is, in its own allegorical way, a method of understanding how mind fits with world and how spirit fits with substance. Thus when Akenside writes in his 'Design' that the powers of imagination occupy a 'middle' space between 'the bodily sense and the faculties of moral perception', he means for us to understand the importance of this kind of mediation as a key to understanding the spiritual qualities of the universe. And, importantly, if an exercise in thinking about the imagination (and its pleasures) also tells us about the philosophic fit of mind and world, then art, and especially poetry – as precisely an exercise of the imagination's powers – might be thought of as vitally philosophic activities.

Akenside's meditation on the connections between material and immaterial things, and poetry's relation to those connections, reaches its zenith in subsequent lines in Book III:

> while you view
> The prospect, say, within your chearful breast
> Plays not the lively sense of winning mirth
> With clouds and sunshine chequer'd, while the round
> Of social converse, to th' inspiring tongue
> Of some gay nymph amid her subject train,
> Moves all obsequious? Whence is this effect,
> This kindred pow'r of such discordant things?
> Or flows their semblance from that mystic tone
> To which the new-born mind's harmonious pow'rs
> At first were strung? Or rather from the links
> Which artful custom twines around her frame?
>
> *(III. 300–11)*

The difficulty of Akenside's syntax here belies the relative simplicity of what he is expressing. He observes that when we look out on a dynamically beautiful scene, we experience what Coleridge would later call (in Akensidean mode) the 'swimming sense' (for more on this, see Section 3). This suggests a symmetry of kinds between our 'swimming' souls and the chequer-work of nature. Akenside then asks where this 'effect' comes from, glossing it as the 'kindred pow'r of such discordant things'. This question is later repeated, albeit more strongly, implicating God in the repetition, in the lines used as an epigram to this Element: 'By what fine ties hath GOD connected things / When present in the mind; which in themselves / Have no connection?' (III. 462–4). The 'effect' is the strange parallelism that opens up between the real world and the worlds of our minds; what is being sought, here and elsewhere in the poem, is the cause behind such an effect.

The apparent sense of connection and interconnectedness here explored – not just between material forms, but between material and immaterial beings – can be thought of as a kind of pathetic fallacy. The sensitive spectator, in *Pleasures of Imagination*, looks on the world as a mirror, and experiences a sense of his own emotional state projected on to it, as if it were sympathetic to his mood. In this way, Akenside hopes, we might also learn to be sympathetic to others and hence fine-tune our moral compasses; he writes that the product of ideas 'connected long' by this process is 'an eternal tie / And sympathy unbroken' (III. 314–18). Akenside, in the lines just quoted, once again uses that uncertain term 'semblance' to describe the status of this mirroring: mind and its contents appear or seem to take on the qualities or behaviours of external forms. It could easily be the other way around, and we might just as well be projecting our feelings on to the world in an act of Addisonian delusion; either way, that connection is how it seems to be, and that is where we form our moral selves. In the final lines just quoted, Akenside provides two traditional sources for that apparent power: the 'mystic tone' of the newborn's mind (read 'nature'), or 'artful custom' (read 'culture'). But crucially, these remain in question as definitive sources or causes of the effect described, and the poem would rather flit between art and nature than alight on a fixed answer.

It is art's role in the process of imaginatively forming links between the mind and the world that takes centre stage in the closing movements of *Pleasures of Imagination*. As noted, if the relation between material and immaterial beings is mediated by way of appearances or 'semblance', then art takes on a semblance of its own: it is an appearance of appearances. Later in Book III Akenside returns to the topic of artistic making and poetic composition:

> The various organs of his mimic skill,
> The consonance of sounds, the featur'd rock,
> The shadowy picture and impassion'd verse,
> Beyond their proper pow'rs attract the soul
> By that expressive semblance, while in sight
> O nature's great original we scan
> The lively child of art.
>
> *(III. 414–21)*

The contents of the artist's toolkit – the 'various organs of his mimic skill' – conspire to create something that can attract or cause pleasure 'Beyond their proper pow'rs'. How, though, can poems do something that we are told is beyond their power? The answer is that they borrow a little more power from elsewhere. It is 'by that expressive semblance' that art captures our attention and causes pleasure – not in itself, but by compiling the best images of 'nature's great original'. But there is a pleasurable ambiguity in these lines too: the 'expressive semblance' itself could refer to the appearance of the artwork as a whole – to a poem such as *Pleasures of Imagination* – or to the appearances of nature the poem attempts to mimic. In creating this ambiguity, Akenside creates the possibility of an expressive ability all of art's own, but also suggests it might be entirely subordinate to nature. The 'expressive' quality cannot be located with precision. This phrasing matters too when we recall the lines much earlier in Book III in which 'searchless nature o'er the sense of man' diffuses a charm that allows him 'to behold, in lifeless things, / The inexpressive semblance of himself' (III. 280–2). The poem moves, and moves us with it, from the *inexpressive* semblances of our minds, contained by our own minds, to the *expressive* semblances offered, or perhaps simply alluded to, by art. Does art raise us above the expressive capabilities of mere 'lifeless things', or is there a life behind those things that furnishes our minds with its own expressive images? The pleasure, for Akenside, is in the contemplation of such things and in the not knowing.

What this section has shown is that Akenside's sense of what it is for the imagination to offer us 'pleasure' rests in the mediating role of the imagination itself, between material and immaterial things and between the mind and the world. Pleasure, for Akenside, is the play of images and appearances, and to that extent 'pleasure' is a product of a set of poetic practices uncoverable in Pope's *Essay on Man*. The way the world seems to us may very well not be how it is at all, but exploration of that uncertainty yields pleasurable rewards. That is also a description of the 'truth' of poetry: not of the ascertaining of facts or the unfolding of philosophical syllogisms, but of an attentiveness paid to the way things seem to be, to us as subjective spectators, in the world's capacity as appearance. Further, the imagination itself, as a mediator and connective faculty, is singularly well placed to illustrate the hidden ways in which mind and world connect, even if we can never truly experience such a connection as knowledge. What we find, then, in *Pleasures of Imagination* is a poetic conception of true: truth as we experience it is something always shifting, something that flickers into and out of being, and yet beyond the frame of our ordinary perceptions we can sense or feel the bigger connections between us and the spiritual world. Crucially, poetry is the best way in which the imagination can offer us fleeting images of such truths, or what Akenside would call 'expressive semblances'. What must be kept in mind, and what Akenside wants us to never lose sight of, is that semblances themselves are only ever subjectively experienced phenomena – the way the world 'seems' to our peculiar and particular minds. Whether by conscious effort or not, Akenside was an inheritor of Pope's poetics as exemplified by *Essay on Man*, a poem that mediates on the truth that the world is only as it appears to us and that explores that notion through the appearances of poetry. And, as the remainder of this Element shows, Akenside's own poem was to prove influential to the school of poetry that would raise issues of semblance to a central feature of art: Romanticism.

3 'There to Read the Transcript of Himself': Coleridge, Akenside, and the Esemplastic Imagination

Samuel Taylor Coleridge was born in 1772, two years after the death of Akenside. That same year, the greatly revised *Pleasures of Imagination* was first published in its five-book form as part of Akenside's collected *Poems*. More than a dozen versions of the poem had already been published before Akenside died, and the 1772 *Poems* was the first of a further dozen collected works to appear before the end of the century. It remained a bestseller and a respected work for the next generation of readers and poets and thus, by the time Coleridge was developing his own voice as a poet, he would quite naturally turn to Akenside's poem as he also would to figures like Spenser and Shakespeare. The key difference, for Coleridge, was that Akenside was a recent addition to the canon of major poets whose works took up ideas that were still very much being discussed after Akenside's death; further, Coleridge would come to see the experiments in blank-verse poetics that Akenside exemplified as not yet fully exhausted. As this section will show, it was for these key reasons that Akenside became a powerful source for Coleridge in the development of his distinctive poetic voice, in the period in the mid-1790s when he was on the path that would lead him to William Wordsworth, to the compos- ition of the *Lyrical Ballads* collection, and to poetic greatness. It was of *Lyrical Ballads* that Coleridge famously theorized the 'suspension of disbelief' that is part of the pact made between reader and artwork, but less famously he also remarked that such suspension is what permits poetry its 'human interest and a semblance of truth', and truth's appearance was always a key concern to Coleridge.[73] Coleridge's use of Akensidean images, ideas, and verse practices is thus an incisive example of how Romanticism took up and responded to *Pleasures of Imagination* more generally, and it is illustrative of the ways in which Akenside was a crucial bridge between high Augustan aesthetics and the major works of the Romantics.

As early as 1796 Coleridge was boasting to the radical John Thelwall that he himself had room in his head to admire both 'the *head* and fancy of Akenside,

---

[73] Samuel Taylor Coleridge, *Biographia Literaria*, in *Samuel Taylor Coleridge: The Major Works*, ed. H. J. Jackson (Oxford: Oxford University Press, 2000), p. 314.

and the *heart* and fancy of Bowles'.[74] Clearly an opposition is implied between the head of Akenside and the heart of William Lisle Bowles, though that opposition is not immediately clear – it could be that, through the parcelling out of heart and head, Coleridge finds a cooler rationalism in Bowles's work and a comparatively strong strain of affectivity in Akenside. Either way, Coleridge's work of the period is marked by its engagement with Akenside's verse, and in fact there are verbal parallels between Akenside and Coleridge that predate the letter to Thelwall. Harriet Jump, for one, has taken pains to detail the extraordinary degree of debt to and citation of Akenside in Coleridge's political writings from 1795 onwards, and finds that 'echoes, quotations, imitations and borrowings from Akenside's work ... occur with startling frequency in letters, notebooks, poems and lectures' of the period.[75] Foremost amongst the material used in Coleridge's lectures is a celebrated early example of Coleridge's empirical belief that God presents himself to the human senses through the symbolical structure of nature:

> [T]he existence of the Deity, and his Power and his Intelligence are manifested, and I could weep for the deadened and petrified Heart of that Man who could wander among the fields in a vernal Noon or summer Evening and doubt his Benevolence! The Omnipotent has unfolded to us the Volume of the World, that there we may read the Transcript of himself. In Earth or Air the meadow's purple stores, the Moons mild radiance, or the Virgins form Blooming with rosy smiles, we see pourtrayed the bright Impressions of the eternal Mind.[76]

This invocation of natural beauty as a proof of benevolence is arresting, not least because it arranges as prose images taken from *Pleasures of Imagination* to an exact degree. Speaking of the higher minds who can most readily perceive God's presence, Akenside writes:

> To these the Sire Omnipotent unfolds
> The world's harmonious volume, there to read
> The transcript of Himself. On every part
> They trace the bright impressions of his hand:
> In earth or air, the meadow's purple stores,
> The moon's mild radiance, or the virgin's form
> Blooming with rosy smiles, they see portray'd
> That uncreated beauty, which delights
> The Mind Supreme.
>
> *(I. 99–107)*

---

[74] Letter to John Thelwall, 17 December 1796, in Samuel Taylor Coleridge, *Collected Letters of Samuel Taylor Coleridge*, ed. E. L. Griggs, 6 vols. (Oxford: Clarendon, 1956–71), vol. 1, p. 279.

[75] Jump, 'High Sentiments of Liberty', p. 207.

[76] Samuel Taylor Coleridge, *Lectures 1795 on Politics and Religion*, ed. Lewis Patton and Peter Mann (Princeton, NJ: Princeton University Press, 1971), p. 94.

With only mild adjustments of pronouns or descriptors for God ('eternal Mind' for the more ambiguous 'uncreated beauty'), Coleridge reproduces Akenside's verses in his lecture notes. It cannot be known how such words were delivered by Coleridge nor how they were received by his audience – if, for example, Coleridge performed the words knowingly as lines of verse, or if his audience could have been expected to recognize lines of such a well-known poem. At any rate, they show that Coleridge looked to Akenside's poetry not just for well-balanced words and images of nature, but for a persuasive restatement of the argument that God can be perceived, by the well-trained eye, within his own works – that nature's appearances form a kind of text authored by God that proves their author's presence. These lines, as Coleridge recognized, carry particular argumentative weight within Akenside's poem, arguing as they do that there are 'higher' types of humans who enjoy greater access to God through nature – poet-philosophers, essentially – but also because they appear as a crucial link within the argument for pleasure as an end to imaginative or intellectual activity. Man in his empirical mode is 'imprinted' on by Nature, and in these lines Akenside reveals the ultimate possibility of such a model of print publication: that the transcript of God can be copied once more into our own minds and be represented there as knowledge. By bringing focus to these lines, Coleridge reveals early on that he was aware of the highest pleasures that could be born of the Akensidean imagination.

The rhetoric of nature as God's 'transcript' was an important one for Coleridge in his early poetry and it rapidly became suffused with his readings in philosophy. Beyond simply restating any traditional account of a religious 'Book of Nature', Coleridge synthesized his reading of empirical and associationist philosophers – chiefly, in the mid-1790s, Berkeley and Hartley – with the aesthetics of *Pleasures of Imagination*, finding, for instance, that 'all that meets the bodily sense' is 'Symbolical, one mighty alphabet'.[77] An important stepping stone in the development of this idea, as well as the first poem that Coleridge himself deemed a major achievement,[78] is the blank-verse theodicy *Religious Musings* of 1796. In that poem Coleridge writes of 'the great / Invisible (by symbols only seen)', pursuing the idea of nature as a language through a discourse of symbolism that he would develop across his career. The title of *Religious Musings* directly conveys the conceit of the poem: it is a staging of loosely structured thoughts that, taken as a whole, express something of the poet's philosophy of religion. Its subtitle, in its published form, calls

---

[77] Akenside, *The Destiny of Nations*, in *Poetical Works*, I. i. p. 280. Henceforth, all other citations to Coleridge's poems refer to the texts of *Samuel Taylor Coleridge: The Major Works* (Oxford: Oxford University Press, 2000).

[78] See Coleridge, *Collected Letters*, vol. 1, pp. 197, 203, 205.

it 'a desultory poem', contributing to the poem's aesthetic of an unplanned or essayistic sense of meandering. In this sense, the poem is significant in Coleridge's oeuvre precisely because it 'represents the sort of poetry he now intended to cultivate', as Lewis Patton notes in his introduction to Coleridge's *Watchman* essays in which parts of *Religious Musings* originally appeared.[79] It marks, in other words, the beginning of the poetized 'system of philosophy' that Coleridge would reflect upon as his life's work and that he would also credit himself with inspiring in the works of Wordsworth.[80]

Tellingly, when setting out on his career as a philosophic poet, Coleridge chose as a motto for the original complete version of *Religious Musings*, published in his 1796 *Poems*, lines adapted from the 1772 text of *Pleasures of Imagination*:

> What tho' first
> In years unseason'd, I attun'd the lay
> To idle Passion and unreal Woe?
> Yet serious Truth her empire o'er my song
> Hath now asserted; Falsehood's evil brood,
> Vice and deceitful Pleasure, she at once
> Excluded, and by Fancy's careless toil
> Drew to the bitter cause![81]

That 'careless toil' is surely redolent of Coleridge's own 'desultory Poem' and his inspiration from Akenside is clear: Coleridge too seeks a song that lies under the imperial rule of 'serious Truth', which acts as a filter between the promised pleasures of the imagination and the falsehoods of the (apparently very similar) 'deceitful Pleasure'. 'Song' is Coleridge's own added word, not Akenside's, and it foreshadows the term 'philosophic Song' Wordsworth would come to use to describe the fitness of blank verse for the kinds of thinking he and Coleridge eventually attempted in their poetry. Coleridge's concern here, as he quotes from *Pleasures of Imagination*, is certainly with thought and thinking, and with how blank verse might promote certain kinds of philosophical activities.

Like *Pleasures of Imagination*, *Religious Musings* opens with a prose 'argument' that outlines the main contours of its narrative: the death and resurrection of Christ, the form of the individual human mind, the structure of modern society and government, the French Revolution, and the Christian doctrine of

---

[79] Samuel Taylor Coleridge, *The Watchman*, ed. Lewis Patton (Princeton, NJ: Princeton University Press, 1970), p. xlviii.

[80] See Samuel Taylor Coleridge, *Table Talk*, ed. Carl Woodring, 2 vols. (Princeton, NJ: Princeton University Press, 1990), vol. 1, pp. 307–8.

[81] Samuel Taylor Coleridge, *Poems on Various Subjects* (Bristol: J. Cottle, 1796), p. 135.

redemption. It is a melting pot of different ideas that Coleridge was pulling in from his varied reading in the period, and though the poem is only a little more than four hundred lines in its finished form, the presence of an 'argument' gloss alone indicates that Coleridge may well have had grander ambitions for it. There are a number of verbal echoes of Akenside in the poem, from the recurring use of epithets such as 'Sire', 'omnipotent', and indeed 'omnipresent Sire' for God, and the word 'blaze' to describe the endless intermingling of material forms under God's instruction. More specifically, though, Coleridge once again draws on Akenside's rhetoric of natural appearances and God's appearance in nature in his own description of 'the Almighty'. As in the 1795 lectures, the 'vernal mead' (which is a shorthand for 'meadow' that conveniently satisfies Coleridge's metre) and the stars, sun, and sea are all 'fair' and will 'True impress each of their creating Sire' – in other words, those forms will print on human minds the knowledge of their own maker. Yet there is a distinction to be made between Akenside's and Coleridge's visions, though both draw on Lockean principles of literalized 'impressions'; for Coleridge, God can also act independently of nature when impressing himself upon us, though for Akenside, he acts solely through natural forms. Coleridge writes that none of the ocean, sky, earth, or sun have:

> E'er with such majesty of pourtraiture
> Imaged the supreme beauty uncreate,
> As thou, meek Saviour!
>
> *(20–2)*

The strongly Akensidean phrase 'beauty uncreate' (recall Akenside's God's 'uncreated beauty') is here categorically distinct from the Saviour himself. This would suggest the possibility of a knowledge of God that bypasses the senses so that, even if he is 'by symbols only seen', he may well be experienced and known by other means. Despite this distinction Coleridge's phrasing is clearly and deliberately lifted from *Pleasures of Imagination* and he is engaging with Akenside's ideas as he takes them up.

Religious Musings is tied to a number of subsequent poems that are central within Coleridge's body of work by the language of appearances it develops, but also by the more specific phraseology of plasticity. At the poem's climax, and at the arrival of the doctrine of redemption, Coleridge offers the following image of the Holy Spirit:

> And ye of plastic power, that interfused
> Roll through the grosser and material mass
> In organizing surge! Holies of God!
>
> *(405–7)*

That 'plastic power' is lifted almost wholesale from Book III of *Pleasures of Imagination*, as the 'child of Fancy' surveys the world around him:

> By degrees the mind
> Feels her young nerves dilate: the plastic powers
> Labour for action: blind emotions heave
> His bosom; and with loveliest frenzy caught,
> From earth to heaven he rolls his daring eye,
> From heaven to earth.
>
> *(III. 380–5)*

It is *almost* lifted wholesale because Coleridge clearly allots the active powers of plasticity to the spiritual presence in nature and not to the perceiver's mind – which, true to his reading of the empiricists and of Hartley, remains passive in its interactions with the world. Akenside prefers his recurrent language of labour, but the effect is the same in both poets: there is a malleable and ever-shifting power in nature that, just as it reshapes itself in and between different forms, so it reshapes our minds under the impressions of new experiences. Indeed, James Engell, in *The Creative Imagination*, credits Akenside with popularizing, if not coining, 'plastic powers' as a term for the imagination's creative work, and he traces a lineage of accounts of the imagination through the eighteenth century which connects Akenside to Coleridge.[82]

In twentieth-century criticism, Akenside's notable uses of the word 'plastic' have received much attention, not just because of the remarkable model of mind he appears to develop in response to the active universe, but also because the word 'plastic' itself has evolved far beyond Akenside's use. Paul H. Fry, working through the findings of Wimsatt and Beardsley's seminal essay 'The Intentional Fallacy', offers Akenside's use of 'plastic' as a case study in the notion that 'the history of words *after* a poem is written may contribute meanings' to the poem itself; as Fry notes, 'everybody knows that Akenside didn't mean polymers', yet we can speculate on how such a reading, freed from intentionality, might contribute to a sense of 'formal richness' in the poem.[83] Whether or not we agree with this methodological approach and its local findings, the example held up – of God's 'plastic arm' as he shapes and restructures the world – does show that plasticity was a key idea for Akenside precisely because it cuts between material and immaterial things, and, by so doing, it made immaterial substances more readily imaginable and appreciable

---

[82] James Engell, *The Creative Imagination* (Cambridge, MA: Harvard University Press, 1981), p. 45.

[83] Paul H. Fry, *Theory of Poetry*, (New Haven, CT: Yale University Press, 2012), p. 67; W. K. Wimsatt Jr and M. C. Beardsley, 'The Intentional Fallacy', *The Sewanee Review*, vol. 54, no. 3 (1946), pp. 468–88.

in an increasingly materialistic age. This was an aspect of the poem to which Coleridge was well attuned, and Coleridge's own reading of Akenside is itself instructional when thinking about influence, reception, and the question of intentionality in great poetry.

Coleridge's early borrowing, in *Religious Musings*, of the term 'plastic powers' set in motion the beginnings of his mature theory of the imagination and of the imagination's pleasures, which was not to be fully realized until the completion of *Biographia Literaria* in 1817. Chapter 10 of that work deals in the 'imagination or plastic power' and opens with the coinage of a new word: *esemplastic*, or 'to shape into one'.[84] Coleridge's model of the imagination is, as Richard C. Sha notes, an effort to bring together the materiality of the body (and of the objects the body perceives) with the substance of its thought.[85] It is *'esem'*-plastic in nature because it synthesizes the ideas it receives as well as bends under the pressures of those ideas – it participates in a process of shaping and being shaped. Sha further notes that Akenside's model of the imagination plays a crucial role in the development of what he calls the 'Material Immateriality' of the imagination in the eighteenth century, as Akenside uniquely 'placed the imagination between bodily sense and moral perception'.[86] There is thus a verbal parallel with Akenside's work in Coleridge's coinage of the 'esemplastic power' but also a clear sign of debt to Akenside's poetic philosophy in this cornerstone of Coleridgean theory: the imagination in essence operates between perceived objects and ideas in our minds, subjects and objects, God and his followers, and it is this intermediary function, dealing as it does in natural appearances, that Coleridge takes for himself from *Pleasures of Imagination*.

Biographia Literaria is also the text in which Coleridge posits that pleasure is the chief end of poetry, a finding which has obvious resonances with Akenside's poem. Coleridge writes, in an attempt to define poetic writing against other forms, that 'a poem is that species of composition, which is opposed to works of science, by proposing for its immediate object pleasure, not truth; and from all other species (having this object in common with it) it is discriminated by proposing to itself such delight from the whole, as is compatible with a distinct gratification from each component part'.[87] Poems can and often do deal in moral or intellectual truths, but those truths are arrived at by chance or accident when the goal in itself is pleasure. This is the goal aimed at by the conspiring elements of metre, poetic language, poetic syntax, and, in many

---

[84] Coleridge, *Biographia Literaria*, p. 239.

[85] Richard C. Sha, 'Toward a Physiology of the Romantic Imagination', *Configurations*, vol. 17, no. 3 (2009), pp. 197– 226, p. 213.

[86] Sha, 'Toward a Physiology of the Romantic Imagination', p. 206.

[87] Coleridge, *Biographia Literaria*, p. 317.

cases, rhyme. The truths of a 'desultory' poem like *Religious Musings*, there-fore, should be received as all the more potent and significant given that they were discovered – apparently – by chance. In the preface to the 1796 *Poems* in which the Akenside-inspired *Religious Musings* first appeared, Coleridge gives a clearer sense of how poetry might generate pleasure from past experiences: 'The communicativeness of our nature leads us to describe our own sorrows; in the endeavour to describe them intellectual activity is exerted; and by a benevolent law of our nature from intellectual activity a pleasure results which is gradually associated and mingles as a corrective with the painful subject of the description.'[88] Poetry is a form of coping in these prefatory remarks whereby sorrows are made bearable by way of a 'corrective' pleasure.[89] It is no stretch to suggest that this pleasure, born of 'a benevolent law of our own nature', relates strongly to Akenside's imaginative pleasures – the synthesizing faculty that allows us to see our semblance in God's active presence in nature. In this light, poetry itself is a necessary part of human sociability, one that responds to our 'communicativeness' – as both a desire to be understood and to understand other humans, but also to commingle with natural forms as in Akenside's poem – as well as our need to overcome sorrow by understanding negative experiences within the larger context of intellectual pleasure. To this end, Coleridge's theory of poetry seems to stem out of the same body of ideas that animates Akenside's theodicy: that negative events are simply instances of variety within a larger, positive whole. Notably, both Akenside's and Coleridge's language of parts and whole and the fit between the two owe much to Pope's similar rhetoric in *Essay on Man*.

Coleridge asserts in *Religious Musings* that God's 'plastic power' tends to 'Roll through the grosser and material mass / In organizing surge!'. The vocabulary Coleridge deploys around that plastic power is significant, and not just because Akenside also uses a 'rolling' image of divine force in close proximity to his own plastic power. It is significant because it connects the early theological speculations of *Religious Musings* with a better-known sub-junctive Romantic excursion:

> And what if all of animated nature
> Be but organic harps diversely framed,
> That tremble into thought, as o'er them sweeps
> Plastic and vast, one intellectual breeze,
> At once the Soul of each, and God of All?
>
> *(44–8)*

---

[88] Samuel Taylor Coleridge, 'Preface', in *Poems on Various Subjects* (Bristol: J. Cottle, 1796).

[89] For more on the thesis that 'rhythm-making is what we do to cope with the world', see Alexander Freer, 'Rhythm As Coping', *New Literary History*, vol. 46, no. 3 (2015), pp. 549–68.

These lines mark the central speculative image of *Effusion XXXV* of 1795, more commonly known today by the name of the musical object at the poem's centre, the Eolian Harp. The poem's narrator imagines what it might mean if the wind that plays across the passive harp – notably, a 'desultory breeze' (14), in connection with the movement of the 'musings' in *Religious Musings* – was in fact a vital 'intellectual breeze' that feeds and fuels all things, including the human mind. Any sense of the adoption of a pantheism here, wherein the 'Soul' of things is precisely the same as 'God of All', is kept at bay by that conditioning 'what if ... ?', and the Coleridge of the poem will be recalled to reason by a reproving look from his 'pensive Sara'. But the 'plastic' nature of the intellectual breeze is redolent of Akenside's spiritually infused appearances, as are the 'organic' forms 'diversely framed'. Indeed, as Steve Clark has shown, the notion of 'framing' is one that Akenside puts great pressure on in *Pleasures of Imagination*.[90] It is in 'this outward frame / Of things' that 'the great Artificer portrays / His own immense idea' in the revised *Pleasures of Imagination* (IV. 82–4) – terms that are strikingly Coleridgean. Frames and framing recur again and again in both versions of Akenside's poem, often at crucial stages in the advancement of his larger argument, and the centrality of framing is due to the flexibility of those images – their plasticity – under Akenside's hands. Our minds frame the world as we experience it, giving us images of all that can be said to seem to be; God in turn frames the universe in which our minds sit. Thus all objects are doubly framed and contained, and these overlapping frameworks suspend human agents between objects of contemplation for God and contemplating subjects in their own right. As Clark notes, 'the same word both vindicates the act of making as something worthy of and allowing access to the deity, and serves as a trope of containment, of absolute circumscription'.[91] Akenside's frames at once place limits on experience as well as derestricting what can be known by reason, and that limiting and delimiting simultaneity might remind us of the powers of apparently restrictive verse measures in the period.

To gain a sense of how and why all this matters for Coleridge, consider the following lines from *Pleasures of Imagination*:

> The bloom of nectar'd fruitage ripe to sense,
> And every charm of animated things,
> Are only pledges of a state sincere,
> The integrity and order of their frame,
> When all is well within, and every end
> Accomplish'd.
>
> *(I. 367–72)*

---

[90] Clark, "'To Bless the Lab'ring Mind'", pp. 142–5.
[91] Clark, "'To Bless the Lab'ring Mind'", p. 143.

Here in Akenside's 'animated things' is the prototype for Coleridge's 'animated nature'. Those natural 'things' are here only markers – givers of sights and scents that attest to their own orderly frames and thus to the organizing principle that makes discrete and distinct knowledge of those forms possible. Similarly, mere lines before those Coleridge copied from *Pleasures of Imagination* for his own 1795 lectures on religion (those concerning the transcript of the 'Sire Omnipotent'), Akenside writes of 'the breath / Of life informing each organic frame' (I. 73–4); here 'intellectual breeze' is spiritual 'breath of life', but in Coleridge's poem the 'organic harps' that are 'diversely framed' are themselves rolled together as 'organic frame[s]'. What Coleridge would have discovered in Akenside's lines and lines like them was a formulation of his own developing thesis, inspired by readings in idealist and associationist philosophy, that perceived things may very well only be appearances, but they are nevertheless appearances caused by God and as such mark and attest to God's presence before us. Though all the material or organic things of the universe, including human 'things', are indeed 'diversely framed', each is united in being ensouled and operated upon by the selfsame spirit of the universe – what Coleridge calls, in the 'Eolian Harp' in a further echo of Akenside, 'the one life within us and abroad / Which meets all motion and becomes its soul' (26–7).

What has been seen so far furthers the argument put forward by David Vallins that Coleridge and Akenside share an emphasis on 'the pleasure of thought' so vivid that it can seem to transcend 'differences of period, style, and (to some extent) source'.[92] There is, though, a further curious connecting thread that runs through all the instances of Akenside's strongest influence on Coleridge's early and formative works, and that is that they all concern the philosopher George Berkeley. As I have shown elsewhere, Coleridge, who named his second-born son Berkeley, was briefly a sworn disciple of Berkeley's in the mid-1790s,[93] and it is notable that his interest in Akenside overlaps with his appreciation of idealism. A footnote added to *Religious Musings* in the *Poems* of 1796 observes that the verse paragraph that pronounces life a 'vision shadowy of Truth' is 'only intelligible to those, who, like the Author, believe and feel the sublime system of Berkley'.[94] Likewise, in the letter to Thelwall in which he mentioned both Akenside and Bowles, he also expresses himself 'a Berkleian'. And Coleridge would look back on the speculative, subjective

---

[92] Vallins, 'Akenside, Coleridge, and the Pleasures of Transcendence', p. 156.
[93] Chris Townsend, 'Nature and the Language of the Sense: Berkeley's Thought in Coleridge and Wordsworth', *Romanticism*, vol. 25, no. 2 (2019), pp. 129–42.
[94] Coleridge, *Poetical Works*, I. i. p.190.

exercise of *Effusion XXXV* as one written in the Berkleian idealist mould.[95] Coleridge only referred to himself as a 'Berkleian' on one other occasion, and it is one that sheds light on the Akenside–idealism link. In a letter to Southey in 1797, Coleridge adds a note saying, 'You remember, I am a *Berkleian*,' alongside the following lines, which contribute to an early version of what would become 'This Lime-tree Bower My Prison':

> So my friend
> Struck with joy's deepest calm, and gazing round
> On the wide view,† may gaze till all doth seem
> Less gross than bodily, a living Thing
> That acts upon the mind, and with such hues
> As clothe the Almighty Spirit, when he makes
> Spirits perceive his presence!
>
>   *(20–6)*[96]

The scene at hand represents an experience of the world as *appearance*: everything in the scene 'doth seem' less gross than bodily, but the word 'seem' itself tempers the remainder of the paragraph at hand; there is no clear way to distinguish between what seems to be and what really is. This is a rhetorical-poetic trick that would become central to Coleridge's aesthetics as his works matured, and as he and Wordsworth set about composing the works that would comprise the *Lyrical Ballads* collections of 1798 which would cement their reputations as leading poets of their generation. The experience in part belongs to Coleridge's reading of idealism, as real objects become indistinguishable from objects of perceptions and what we see is what we get. But it equally reveals the extent of Coleridge's debt to Akenside, from whom he borrowed not just the philosophic possibilities of 'serious' blank verse, but also the slipperiness of appearances as they populate *Pleasures of Imagination*. The world as it 'seems to be' in Coleridge, which is so central to his philosophic poetry, is in large part a borrowing from Akenside's poetic take on the 'Appearances in the World around Us'; in that sense it continues a kind of poetized Enlightenment narrative begun in the works of Pope.

What matters here, in the realization of the extent to which Coleridge's philosophic poetry is indebted to Akenside in terms of metrical structure, images, and ideas, is that Akenside himself was drawing on Pope's *Essay on Man*. Akenside's masterstroke though, as Coleridge would see it, was realizing the full potential of blank verse – that is, Akenside jettisoned the restrictions of the rhyming couplet and so delimited verse-borne philosophy. Coleridge saw

---

[95] Samuel Taylor Coleridge, *Lectures 1818–1819: On the History of Philosophy*, ed. J. R. de J. Jackson (Princeton, NJ: Princeton University Press, 2001), p. 557.

[96] Coleridge, *Collected Letters*, vol. 1, p. 335n.

himself as continuing that tradition, which was still novel by the time he was embarking on his career as a poet. It is a tradition fundamentally rooted in and not opposed to the structures of Neoclassical verse. The idea that poetry, as a representational mode, can itself parallel a more primal form of representation – the receiving of images in our minds which serve to represent ideas in the world, or what Coleridge characterizes as ideas traversing an 'indolent and passive brain' in the 'Eolian Harp' (41) – was one Coleridge took from Akenside, but it has its foundations in Pope's play of natural and artificial languages. I want to underscore here the fact that Coleridge's verse philosophizing, on the subject of organically framed minds and the appearances that populate them, is itself an organic continuation of a high Augustan idea: that the structures and sounds of poetry can echo its sense, that poems can appear to be reorganizations of thought which is itself a restructuring of the external world, and that poetry, as a kind of appearance in itself, is singularly adapted to transcribing the appearances of the world. That aptness is in part because poetry's appearances are not always the same as reality. That lesson was passed on to Coleridge, for whom poetry serves to turn experiences of sorrow into pleasures of the imagination; there is a linear progression from high Augustan to Romantic that calls the lie to any overly simplistic account of opposition between the two. Seen up close and in proximity to Akenside's work, Coleridge's Romanticism is not at odds with Neoclassical poetry nor in deviation from it, but is rather a progression on its major themes. Having seen that idea at work in Coleridge's poetry, the final section of this book now turns to Romanticism more broadly, to understand Akenside's wider influence in the period and his role as a bridge between poetry of the early 1800s and of the 1700s.

4 Akenside's Romanticism: Wordsworth, Keats, and Imaginative Pleasures

Coleridge was one of Akenside's best readers in the Romantic period, and, certainly during the mid-1790s, he was one of the most dedicated of respondents to *Pleasures of Imagination*. But Akenside's poem, at least in its original version, was hugely popular across the eighteenth century, and it was enjoyed practically as important a role for serious readers of poetry in the early decades of the nineteenth century as it had been in the latter 1740s. The poem cast a long shadow, one that touches upon a number of key Romantic-period writers besides Coleridge and one that influenced the notion we hold today of Romantic poetics. To give a sense of this breadth of influence, of the particular nature of this influence, and how Akenside additionally connects Romanticism to earlier eighteenth-century verse and philosophical cultures, the current section turns to the works of two other major figures of Romanticism to explore their debts to Akenside and his verse-borne philosophy: William Wordsworth and John Keats.

Wordsworth and Keats between them give us a fuller picture of the progression of Romanticism – of the so-called first and second generations of English Romantic poetry and of the disagreements between the two. They also help us understand how the intellectual lineage of which *Pleasures of Imagination* is a part is continued in very different ways and by very different poets. When Wordsworth and Keats met for the first and only time, at Benjamin Robert Haydon's 'immortal dinner' of 1817, the older poet already had much of his best poetry behind him, whilst the younger was on the cusp of the period in which his greatest works would appear. Keats would go on to write, famously, against 'the Wordsworthian or egotistical sublime' – the mode of self-centred nature-poetics Keats found exemplified in Wordsworth, which, like Akenside, transforms nature into a kind of mirror for the self or individual mind.[97] Instead of this, Keats sought an experience of dissolution of selfhood, as a kind of feeling of integration with nature and the world beyond ourselves, however fleeting. This section turns to Wordsworth and then to Keats to show the ways in which each of these apparently contradictory modes – egotistical sublime and self-dissolution – borrow from *Pleasures of Imagination*. More than this, these borrowings connect the poets to the deeper tradition, established in the Augustan era by Addison and Pope, of thinking about natural appearances as consonant with poetic aesthetics, and of thinking about appearances through verse-form poetry. In this spirit, this section, and the main argument of this Element, ends with a meditation on the verse forms exemplified by Wordsworth and Keats – blank verse and the 'cockney' couplet – to connect those ways of writing to the deeper tradition explored in previous section. It also turns to two of the greatest odes by those poets, each of which contains notably Akensidean ideas and images: the 'Ode ("There was a time")' by Wordsworth and Keats's ode 'To a Nightingale'.

In the first of his two-volume work *Wordsworth's Reading*, Duncan Wu offers 1779 as the earliest possible dating of Wordsworth's exposure to Akenside's poetry; he would have been nine years old at the time. Whether or not Wordsworth did read Akenside as early as his school days, there is abundant evidence that he was an appreciator of *Pleasures of Imagination* by his teenage years. The earliest surviving work by Wordsworth, the 'Lines Written As

---

[97] Keats, *Keats's Poetry and Prose*, p. 295.

a School Exercise' of 1785, contain what Wu, amongst other critics, notes is an allusion to Akenside's poem. Wordsworth writes of:

> she who trains the generous British youth
> In the bright paths of fair majestic Truth[98]

These words echo lines from early in Book I of *Pleasures of Imagination*, ones that refer to the spiritual force in nature:

> The guide, the guardian of their lovely sports,
> Majestic TRUTH.
>
> *(I. 22–3)*

Though a simple echo, there is a sense in which this borrowing, and its spiritual guide or 'guardian' figure, is a formative one for Wordsworth. Harriet Jump notes that the narrator of the 1794 version of *An Evening Walk* is at one point 'guided by some hand unseen',[99] and connects that image to a passage from *Pleasures of Imagination*:

> How gladly I recall you well-known seats
> Beloved of old, and that delightful time
> When, all alone, for many a summers day
> I wanderd through your calm recesses, led
> In silence by some powerful hand unseen.
>
> *(V. 41–5)*

The phrases are strikingly similar, and the fact that Wordsworth brings together that 'unseen hand' with the action of a specifically 'guiding' force in nature is suggestive of the influence Akenside's poem had on him. A language of guides and guardians would permeate Wordsworth's later *Prelude*, from the cloud that acts as the poet's guide in the opening lines and onwards. It is also notable how closely Wordsworth follows Akenside's lead in a line from *Lines Written a Few Miles above Tintern Abbey* which describes 'nature and the language of the sense' as 'The guide, the guardian' of the poet's heart (111). Akenside, we saw, appealed to Coleridge in part because his programme of reading nature as a the 'transcript' of God promised to synthesize the methods of empirical philosophy with natural theology, and here, in one of Wordsworth's best-known poems and one that was published during his period of intense collaboration with

---

[98] Ernest De Selincourt and Helen Darbishire, eds., *The Poetical Works of William Wordsworth*, 5 vols. (Oxford: Clarendon, 1940–9), vol. 1, pp. 260–1. Henceforth, all subsequent citations of Wordsworth's poetry refer to the text of *William Wordsworth: The Major Works*, ed. Stephen Gill (Oxford: Oxford University Press, 2008).

[99] Harriet Jump, "'That Other Eye': Wordsworth's 1794 Revisions of 'An Evening Walk'", *The Wordsworth Circle*, vol. 17, no. 3 (1986), pp. 156–63, p. 156.

Coleridge, we find evidence that Wordsworth too found such philosophical inspiration in Akenside.

A major part of Akenside's legacy in Romanticism was more specific than simply the notion that his poem helped continue the popularity of blank verse in the Miltonic tradition (as did other notably eighteenth-century poets, including James Thomson and Edward Young), in that his approach to blank verse was developed in close relation to the philosophical project of *Pleasures of the Imagination*. Further, the way in which part and whole fit in his poem is explored through the fit of particular lines with verses as a whole; to this extent, metre is a guiding force in the poem in a more than metaphorical sense, and it gives a contextualizing form to the many and varied rhythmical arrangements of the poem's line units. I want now to propose that the language of natural-spiritual guidance and guardianship to which Wordsworth was so sensitive in *Pleasures of Imagination* also helped the young poet establish the approach to blank-verse philosophizing that he would make his own within the canon of English literature: metre, in his handling, is itself a kind of unseen guide, one that steers the thought-content of poetry. When Mary Jacobus writes that the works of Akenside 'were peculiarly relevant to the Wordsworth of 1798', she could thus be talking in equal measure about his developing philosophy of nature and about his approach to poetic form.[100] It is the closeness of these two strains of his thinking that I want to trace back to a single source in the works of Akenside.

To understand in brief the enduring connection between Akenside's poetry and Wordsworth's verse thinking, it will be instructive to turn briefly to one of the latter's most celebrated philosophical poems: the 'Ode ('There was a time')'. The poem is a meditation on loss; specifically, it charts the apparent loss of a certain way of seeing the world, couched explicitly in the terms of semblance, as it is experienced in childhood but missing in adulthood:

> There was a time when meadow, grove, and stream,
>   The earth, and every common sight,
>   To me did seem
>   Apparelled in celestial light,
>   The glory and the freshness of a dream.
> It is not now as it hath been of yore; –
>   Turn wheresoe'er I may,
>   By night or day,
> The things which I have seen I now can see no more.
>
>   *(1–9)*

---

[100] Mary Jacobus, *Tradition and Experiment in Wordsworth's Lyrical Ballads (1798)* (Oxford: Clarendon, 1976), p. 53.

Though this theme – of a loss of a sense of 'celestial light' as experienced in childhood – is now considered to be a quintessentially Wordsworthian one, its source appears to lie in *Pleasures of Imagination*. Illustrating the principle of variety as pertaining to natural forms as well as poetry, Akenside writes early in Book I:

> Witness the sprightly joy when aught unknown
> Strikes the quick sense, and wakes each active pow'r
> To brisker measures: witness the neglect
> Of all familiar prospects, tho' beheld
> With transport once; the fond attentive zeal
> Of age, commenting on prodigious things.
> For such the bounteous providence of heav'n,
> In every breast implanting this desire
> Of objects new and strange, to urge us on
> With unremitted labour to pursue
> Those sacred stores that wait the ripening soul,
> In truth's exhaustless bosom.
>
> *(I. 232–44)*

Akenside offers his own prose gloss to these lines in one of the notes that follow the poem:

> It is here said, that in consequence of the love of novelty, objects which at first were highly delightful to the mind, lose that effect by repeated attention to them. But the instance of *habit* is oppos'd to this observation; for *there*, objects at first distasteful are in time render'd intirely agreeable by the repetition of action[101]

The existence of this note marks the lines out as ones that mattered to Akenside, and the interest Wordsworth would have taken in them is clear: things that were once delightful to the senses and to the mind now are no longer delightful. This Wordsworthian theme is a product of our becoming accustomed to the same sights, although, paradoxically, it is by habit that we also develop taste. What this demands, for Akenside, at least in terms of his aesthetics, is the same principle of variety outlined in the 'Design' to the poem: verse, like the objects of the sense, should be constantly surprising in order to be always interesting; '*wonder*', he writes, 'indeed always implies *novelty*, being never excited by common or well-known appearances'.[102]

Thus it is that the 'appearances' at the beginning of Wordsworth's 'Ode' are structured in accordance with Akenside's thought. And they *are* appearances or semblances of truth: everything once *seemed* apparelled in celestial light, but

---

[101] Akenside, *Poetical Works*, p. 156.   [102] Akenside, *Poetical Works*, p. 157.

the world changes because perception has changed. By singling out 'every common sight' at the head of his poem, Wordsworth leaves room for the notion of uncommon sights, ones that might still carry a sense of visionary gleam; he also connects the poem, through that phrase, to Akenside's 'common or well-known appearances'. The 'gleam' of truth that Wordsworth's poem goes on to describe could well be what Akenside describes when he writes 'Nor let that gleam / Of youthful hope that shines upon your hearts, / Be chill'd or clouded (I.387–8), and Wordsworth will borrow similar images for his 'Shades of the prison-house' which 'begin to close / Upon the growing Boy'. Again, Akenside offers the instruction:

> O let thy soul
> Remember, what the will of heav'n ordains
> Is ever good for all; and if for all,
> Then good for thee. Nor only by the warmth
> And soothing sunshine of delightful things,
> Do minds grow up and flourish. Oft misled
> By that bland light, the young and unpractis'd views
> Of reason wander thro' a fatal road,
> Far from their native aim: as if to lye
> Inglorious in the fragrant shade, and wait
> The soft access of ever-circling joys,
> Were all the end of being.
>
> *(II. 548–57)*

The 'remembering' soul recalls the Platonic doctrine of *anamnesis* or recollection on which Wordsworth founded the central affirmation of his ode, that 'that in our embers / Is something that doth live, / That Nature yet remembers / What was so fugitive' (132–5). But as Akenside's passage continues, it goes on to make a strange distinction as it explains how minds – even poetic minds – can be led astray from the moral truths of nature. 'Soothing sunshine' can be displaced by 'that bland light' which characterizes the 'young and unpractis'd views / Of reason'. The false 'fragrant shade', as opposed to daylight, again recalls Plato and the shadows seen in the analogy of the cave in the *Republic*. But the replacement of one kind of light with another will feel immediately familiar to readers of Wordsworth's 'Ode', in which 'celestial light' fades into common 'daylight' (76) – not darkness, not night, but an almost identical and yet crucially changed appearance.

Akenside's distinction between 'bland' light and heavenly sunshine is a product of reasoning: a guiding light that is shone from within, as opposed to the more illuminating 'light of things' (as in Wordsworth's phrase in the *Lyrical Ballads* poem 'Expostulation and Reply'). Wordsworth himself would later pit two kinds of reason against one another in his long philosophic poem *The Prelude*. He describes the abstracting work of the understanding as 'flattering to the young ingenuous mind / Pleased with extremes, and not the least with that / Which makes the human reason's naked self / The object of its fervour' (X. 815–18). These will, however, turn out to be 'reasonings false', but while they last they bring the young poet deep pleasure ('What delight! – / How glorious!'); in this sense, such reasonings follow the blueprint of the youthful 'pleasing errors' Akenside warns against when we rely on our own inward sense and not on external impressions. Wordsworth summarizes this stage of life in Book XI:

> There comes a time when Reason – not the grand
> And simple Reason, but that humbler power
> Which carries on its no inglorious work
> By logic and minute analysis
> Is of all idols that which pleases most
> The growing mind.
>
> *(XI. 123–8)*

In retrospect, the understanding is not 'inglorious' – which, in literal terms, is to say that it does cast some light – but it is clearly weak when compared to 'grand and simple reason'. That second category of the mind Wordsworth will go on to celebrate at the poem's apex, in its guise as the human imagination. Thus in this sense too Wordsworth's poetry reanimates an Akensidean concern and it is notable that the preferable form of imaginative reasoning in *The Prelude* falls on the image of a 'mighty mind', one that 'appeared' to the poet. Once again, an ambiguous appearance – whether as the activity of an object or as an appearance in the mind of the subject – takes centre stage.

The vehicle in which that reanimation takes place is, of course, blank verse in the Miltonic tradition, and it is verse that serves to guide the poet's thought in *The Prelude*. From the opening of *The Prelude* onwards there is a clearly stated theme of guidance: nature acts to guide the growing mind of the poet, to feed and inspire the imagination that will take centre stage in Book XIII; along the way, there are threats to the poet's unmediated access to nature in the forms of book-learning and his formal education at Cambridge, which parallel the 'Shades of the prison-house' that close around the growing boy in the 'Ode ('There was a time')'. *The Prelude* opens as follows:

> Oh there is blessing in this gentle breeze
> That blows from the green fields and from the clouds
> And from the sky: it beats against my cheek,
> And seems half-conscious of the joy it gives.
>
> *(I. 1–4)*

In these lines Wordsworth is concerned above all with naturalism and with the forces of nature. Yet his poem also displays what Abrams influentially called 'natural supernaturalism'.[103] It concerns the fit between mind and world and depends upon an order that underlies apparently contingent experience and that lies behind the apparently disordered forms of the world. The pull of blank-verse rhythm, as Akenside had proved in *Pleasures of Imagination*, was enough to generate a sense of that larger order, that which gives structure to the whole even as the parts pull in their various directions. The blessing of that 'gentle breeze' is the blessing of blank-verse poetry: invisibly, it exerts its inexorable pull over the sense of sentences and leads it towards larger metrical order. As Wordsworth writes mere lines later, 'should the guide I chuse / Be nothing better than a wandering cloud / I cannot miss my way' (I. 17–19). The guide Wordsworth chose for his experiments in philosophic versification when he was composing as a young man in the later 1790s was the principle of varied blank-verse rhythms that was being taken up by, amongst others, the poet Charlotte Smith, and which had been popularized by Akenside. The same principle of guidance and guardianship animates the stately blank verse of *Tintern Abbey*, which, though it ultimately draws inspiration for its rhythms from Milton, appears to arrive at Miltonic poetics via Akenside. There, as in *The Prelude*, it is variety of lines that allows for change and growth – the growth of the poet's mind, the changed states between the first and second visits to the river Wye, as separated by five years. But is the larger structure of verse that binds the poet's days, each to each, and line to line.

John E. Sitter has remarked that Wordsworth's later experiments with philosophical poetry, including the well-known remarks in the 'Prospectus' to the *Excursion* – written in self-consciously 'numerous' or varied verse, and concerning how 'the individual Mind . . . to the external World / Is fitted' – notably reveal debts to Akenside in their images as well as their verse techniques.[104] But a strong influence from Akenside's *Pleasures of Imagination* is also found in the younger poet Keats. Knowledge of Keats's reading in general is limited mainly to those works he mentions in his notes and critical writings – for the most part the great English poets, including Spenser, Shakespeare, and Milton – and to the volumes he owned as listed in a letter by Benjamin Bailey.[105] And despite James Caldwell's confident claim that Keats did indeed 'read Addison and Akenside',

---

[103] Meyer H. Abrams, *Natural Supernaturalism: Tradition and Revolution in Romantic Literature* (New York: Norton, 1973).

[104] 'Prospectus' to *The Excursion*, quoted in Sitter, 'Theodicy at Midcentury', pp. 91–2.

[105] See Hyder Edward Rollins, ed., *The Keats Circle: Letters and Papers* (Cambridge, MA: Harvard University Press, 1965), p. 258.

citation is found wanting there and primary evidence lacking.[106] Yet Keats and Akenside were both, at various times in their lives, poet-physicians and residents of Hampstead in north London, and certainly Keats's close friend and mentor Leigh Hunt knew Akenside's work well, even if he did find in it 'a great deal of second-hand workmanship'.[107] And there is a strong debt to Akenside that is discoverable in myriad close textual parallels and borrowed images, the recognition of which requires attention to individual lines. It has been noted, for example, that there is likely an Akensidean source behind one of Keats's most well-known formulations: that '"Beauty is truth, truth beauty, – that is all / Ye know on earth, and all ye need to know"'.[108] I have included Keats's punctuation in that quotation as it is important to remember that it does not fall within the narrative voice of the poem. Rather, it is reported speech: of the urn, perhaps, or from elsewhere in the history of artistry and poetics, as common wisdom or universal truth. One source for that wisdom lies in Akenside's *Pleasures of Imagination*:

> Thus was beauty sent from heav'n,
> The lovely ministress of truth and good
> In this dark world: for truth and good are one,
> And beauty dwells in them, and they in her,
> With like participation. Wherefore then,
> O sons of earth! would ye dissolve the tye?
>
> *(I. 372–6)*

His wording is less pithy, certainly, but Akenside here rolls together goodness and truth within the concept of heaven-sent beauty. This is the same gesture Akenside would make in Book II of *Pleasures of the Imagination* when considering the potential of poetry, in the guise of the Orphean lyre, to 'piece divine philosophy's retreats', to unite philosophy and poetry under the rubric of 'truth and beauty' (II. 63–8). Notably, Akenside here also forms the rhetorical structure of a chiasmus, as in Keats's more famous example: where Keats folds 'beauty/truth' into 'truth/ beauty', Akenside's runs 'beauty/truth-and-good' to 'truth-and-good/beauty'. What is clear, though, is that Akenside's poem provides a viable model for both the structure and logic for Keats's best-known claim.

It is, however, another of Keats's great odes that best embodies his debt to Akenside. Akenside's own ode 'To the Evening-Star' offers a memorable appearance of the Endymion myth that Keats would make his own in *Endymion* of 1818, in which a sleeping shepherd prince is romanced by the moon. For Geoffrey Hartman, Keats's later ode 'To a Nightingale' is, 'with its

---

[106] James Ralston Caldwell, *John Keats' Fancy* (Ithaca, NY: Cornell University Press, 1945), p. 71.

[107] Leigh Hunt, *The Examiner*, 492 (1 June 1817).

[108] John Buxton, *The Grecian Taste: Literature in the Age of Neo-Classicism, 1740–1820* (London: Palgrave, 1978).

finely repeated darkling moment and green space', a 'fulfillment of Akenside's
"To the Evening Star"'.[109] That poem also, though, bespeaks a debt to *Pleasures
of Imagination*. In *Pleasures of Imagination* a nightingale appears in its classical
form under the name Philomela, at the end of a lengthy verse sequence that
meditates on the respective claims to beauty made by art and by nature. When it
does appear, the language used to describe it and the appearances of beauty
around it are of an order that will feel familiar to readers of Keats:

> When join'd at eve,
> Soft-murm'ring streams and gales of gentlest breath
> Melodious Philomela's wakeful strain
> Attempter, could not man's discerning ear
> Thro' all its tones the symphony pursue.
>
> *(III. 471–5)*

The passage will continue to state that, though man might have difficulties
'pursuing' the subtle birdsong, the song as 'breath divine' will nevertheless
'Steal thro' his veins' and into his heart; what may not greet our senses,
Akenside tells us, might nevertheless meet us as knowledge via subtler feelings.
(Wordsworth would later rhyme 'feeling' with love that is 'stealing' from heart
to heart in the short lyric 'To My Sister', in similar fashion to this passage.) The
movement of the narrator in Keats's 'To a Nightingale' could readily be
described as the 'pursuit' of the birdsong: 'Away! away! for I will fly to thee'.
The 'quiet breath' in Keats's ode repeats the 'gales of gentlest breath' that is the
birdsong in *Pleasures of Imagination*; Keats's 'melodious plot' carries the same
music as 'Melodious Philomela'. 'To a Nightingale's 'murmurous haunt of flies
on summer eves' also echoes Akenside's 'Soft-murm'ring streams', though
Keats's own stream, at the end of the poem, is 'still'. Both poets invoke images
that are apparently of the 'warm South', though Keats's 'foam / Of perilous
seas' is at odds with Akenside's 'caerulean convex of the sea / With equal
brightness and equal warmth' (III. 465–6). The 'wakeful strain' of Akenside's
nightingale leads into the famous Keatsian questions: 'Was it a vision, or
a waking dream? / Fled is that music: – Do I wake or sleep?' Tellingly, only
twenty lines earlier than the appearance of his own nightingale, Akenside poses
a very similar rhetorical question:

> Thou grave censor! say,
> Is beauty then a dream, because the glooms
> Of dulness hang too heavy on thy sense
> To let her shine upon thee?
>
> *(III. 447–50)*

---

[109] Hartman, 'Reflections on the Evening Star', p. 111.

Here are Keats's 'verdurous glooms', the dullness that will lend itself to 'some dull opiate' and the image of a 'dull brain', a numbness of the senses, and beauty that might well be only a dream if we begin to doubt the veracity of our own senses. For Keats, 'there is no light, / Save what from heaven is with the breezes blown'; for Akenside, the man 'Whose eye ne'er open'd on the light of heav'n' (III. 451) might well wrongly suppose there is no truth beyond its own reasoning. In both, true knowledge figures as heavenly light and is posited as the ultimate goal of the poet.

None of this is to suggest that the ode 'To a Nightingale' is a simple reshuffling of the images and elements of one short section of *Pleasures of Imagination* – it is not a permutation on a pre-existing theme, but rather a renewal of and challenge to some of Akenside's central theses. Keats complicates the relationship between senses, mind, and the external world – the Akensidean discourse of appearances – by calling into question any easy distinction between what Akenside calls a 'raptur'd vision' (III. 452) and the visionariness of a dream. In doing so he reflects, for instance, the Kantian critique of dogmatic idealism, as being unable to distinguish between the contents of a dream and waking life – 'do I wake or sleep?' is in that respects a pertinent philosophical question to ask of the world's appearances.[110] But Keats is clearly engaging with Akenside's poetry as did Wordsworth, taking seriously its philosophizing and expanding upon its thinking in his own verse-form engagement with the nightingale. Following the verbal echoes between *Pleasures of the Imagination* up to the concluding questions of 'To a Nightingale', Keats appears most interested in that aspect of Akenside's thinking that Wordsworth recast as a distinction between the work of reason and the imagination, wherein there is the risk of misreading the ideas we see in the world in accordance with our own fanciful ideas – where, in effect, the contents of our minds eclipse our view of the world. Kirk Fabel has this risk in mind when he writes, of Akenside, that 'opinion can mislead the percipient away from the True when "fancy cheats the intellectual eye". A tension therefore arises between reason and fancy which Akenside, unlike Addison, endows with a negative capacity'.[111] This is one of the strangest and most striking aspects of *Pleasures of the Imagination*, and it bears repeating in the context of Akenside's Romantic readership: where Addison saw the imagination as a threat to truth, Akenside realized that the imagination, even when it leads us momentarily away from the world of fixed truths, will tend to lead us towards pleasure. To be misled in this sense is to create the opportunity of losing and then re-finding truth – that pleasurable frisson noted in Section 2 of this Element. Keats finds such

---

[110] See Immanuel Kant, *Prolegomena to Any Future Metaphysics*, ed. Beryl Logan (London: Routledge, 1996), p. 61.

[111] Fabel, 'Location of the Aesthetic', p. 62.

a pleasure in the song of the nightingale: 'thou art pouring forth thy soul abroad /
In such an ecstasy!' That archaism, 'art', offers a creative pun; and, following on
from a mention of 'soft names in many a mused rhyme', Keats primes us to think
about the leading and misleading pleasures of verse itself. Though it may not be
a direct path towards truth, by opening us up to pleasure we experience something
analogous to the discovery of God in nature; as in *Pleasures of Imagination*,
song – as birdsong or bard-song – forms a structural analogy to the leading and
misleading appearances of the world. The section of *Pleasures of Imagination*
Keats drew from for 'To a Nightingale' reflects precisely the power of the poet to
reproduce, in small scale, the experience of spiritualized nature and its appearances; in fact, the lines concern the 'expressive semblance' of art as it represents
natural beauty:

> The various organs of his mimic skill,
> The consonance of sounds, the featur'd rock,
> The shadowy picture and impassion'd verse,
> Beyond their proper pow'rs attract the soul
> By that expressive semblance, while in sight
> Of nature's great original we scan
> The lively child of art; while line by line,
> And feature after feature we refer
> To that sublime exemplar whence it stole
> Those animating charms.
>
> *(III. 415–24)*

What we find here is an exemplary statement of Akenside's theory of versification and verse-form mimesis, right at the moment when Keats saw fit to borrow
most heavily from *Pleasures of Imagination*. Sound, image, and metre conspire
to work beyond their own 'proper pow'rs', to enact a sense of natural beauty –
like an ode reconstructing mellifluous birdsong. As in Wordsworth's *Prelude*,
nature is the guide to poetic imagery, but the form of verse is the guide to
thinking: 'line by line' of the poem maps on to 'feature after feature' of the
'sublime exemplar' that is nature. This is a quintessential example of the nature
poetics that would dominate Romantic writings, but not only was it published
some fifty years before the heyday of Romanticism and the publication of the
Lyrical Ballads – and more than seventy years before Keats's odes – it is also
a model of poetics structured in accordance with principles taken from that
highest of high Augustans, Alexander Pope.

I have suggested that Wordsworth and Keats both found a fusion of natural
imagery and poetic practice in Akenside's *Pleasures of Imagination* that was

helpful to each in the establishment of their own verse writings. The originality of those writings should not be lost or forgotten when considering such lines of influence, great though those influences are; there has not been another Wordsworth or Keats since those writers and there was not a like writer before them. Yet in thinking about the way the world appears, and in allowing verse to interact and interfere with the structure of that thinking, both Wordsworth and Keats reveal a crucial debt to Akenside that in turn came to Akenside from Pope's poetics. In Wordsworth, this is the development of a blank-verse style that would allow the metre to guide the myriad lines and images of the poem; in Keats, it is the reproduction of natural beauty, in the form of birdsong, within a verse medium that allows him to pry open the question of the relation of appearances to mere semblances – to the question of whether one is awake or sleeping, and how we could possibly know the difference. That activity of not knowing is what Keats came to call – famously, and influentially – 'Negative Capability', and in closing this section I want to suggest that this too might be counted as one of the imagination's foremost pleasures in an Akensidean sense, and hearkens back to Pope's poetics of uncertainty in *Essay on Man*. Interestingly, Kirk Fabel calls Akenside's take on delusion or illusory appearances his 'negative capacity';[112] unlike Addison, Akenside wants to allow the mind to stray from its immediate objects, to take pleasure in being led and misled in what Coleridge would call a 'desultory' poetic exploration of truth and untruth. As in Pope, certainty is less important than a dynamic mental capacity, where the possibility of different and competing forms of knowledge can be kept open. For Keats, negative capability is the ability to entertain conflicting or unresolved thoughts 'without irritable reaching after fact'.[113] Akenside too promotes a kind of knowing that does not depend upon fact but upon feeling and that thus can entertain pleasure as a stepping stone towards truth. What I've charted across this section is the relation of the mode of unresolved knowing, which Keats crystallized in his 'Negative Capability' remarks, to the shifting play of appearances in Romanticism, in Akenside, and in Pope alike. From Popean Neoclassical verse, through Akenside, and on to Coleridge, Wordsworth, and Keats, we see evolution of a poetics that is concerned above all with how the world seems to be – of how the world greets us as appearance, how it appears to us and for us, and how subjective experience and not objective reality is the condition for our knowing.

---

[112] Fabel, 'Location of the Aesthetic', p. 62.

[113] John Keats, 'Letter to George and Tom Keats, December 21, 27?, 1817', in *Keats's Poetry and Prose*, ed. Jeffrey N. Cox (New York: Norton, 2009), p. 109.

Conclusion: Things Connected

There is a stronger tradition of thinking of Romantic poetry as concerned first and foremost with appearances within German thought than there is in English. In 1790, Immanuel Kant, in *The Critique of the Power of Judgment*, made an influential distinction between *Schein* and *Erscheinung* – between 'mere semblances' and the world's actual 'appearance'. This was strongly attached to Kant's distinction between the noumenal and phenomenal world in that work, or the world as it really is and the world as we experience it. G. F. W. Hegel took up this terminology in his *Lectures on Aesthetics* to define poetry, and especially Romantic lyric poetry, as concerned, first and foremost, with semblance: poetry deals in appearances of the world, but also creates its own 'semblance' – its appearance of a real voice speaking, of a real event taking place, of a reality parallel to the real world, all of which is in fact predicated upon fiction.[114] More than a century and a half later, the interplay of 'semblance' and 'expression' (the speaking of truth, separate from mimetic representations of reality) was the cornerstone of Theodor Adorno's magnum opus, *Aesthetic Theory*, and its discussion of the social function of art and poetry.[115] Between Hegel and Adorno, Nietzsche wrote of *Schein* as the fundamental trick of dramatic tragic works: to create the appearance of an event whilst attesting to their own status as *mere appearances* so that we can at once subscribe to the fiction of the play whilst remaining disinterested from its events.[116] For all of these writers, the poem's status as appearance is central to how it functions and this discovery can be traced back to Romantic-period thought.

No such explicit account of semblance exists in the English tradition of aesthetics, and yet as this Element has shown, there is grounds for thinking of a preoccupation with philosophical appearances as a major product of eighteenth-century thought, especially thought that occurred in poetry. From Alexander Pope's major philosophical poem *Essay on Man*, with its attempt to display in verse the structure of a universe ordered under God, to Wordsworth's less generalizing but similarly empirical nature poetics in *The Prelude*, poetry, in its capacity as a special kind of appearance, was increasingly taken up across the long eighteenth century as a vehicle fit for thinking through the relation of mind and world and how the world appears to be. Though Neoclassical verse is often taken to be at odds with Romanticism, with the latter seen as a hostile reaction against the former, there is in fact an organic

---

[114] See especially the translator's note on *Schein* in Hegel, *Lectures on Aesthetics*, I. p. 4n1.

[115] Theodor W. Adorno, *Aesthetic Theory*, trans. Robert Hullot-Kentor (London: Continuum, 2004).

[116] Friedrich Nietzsche, *The Birth of Tragedy and Other Writings*, ed. Raymond Geuss and Ronald Speirs (Cambridge: Cambridge University Press, 1999).

development between both movements, traceable through evolving attitudes to versified philosophizing. At the centre of the knot connecting Neoclassicism to Romanticism was Akenside's profoundly influential bestselling poem, *The Pleasures of Imagination.*

Nowhere is the theorization of poetry as 'appearance' more apparent in the eighteenth century than in Akenside's prose 'Design' to the poem, where he expounds the pleasures 'of the nature of imitation itself': of the 'various and complicated resemblance existing between several parts of the material and immaterial worlds, which is the foundation of metaphor and wit'.[117] Nature is a shifting set of appearances and verse, as a sequence of varying unrhymed lines at the hands of Akenside, forms an imitation of the structure of reality: endlessly changing at the level of particulars, but organized and 'framed', in Akenside's favoured term, by God at the general level. As Pope was at pains to refer part back to whole time and again across his *Essay on Man*, utilizing the rhyming couplet to underscore the fit between an individual 'soul' and the organization of the whole, Akenside adapted this conception of versified philosophy to blank verse, checking line against verse time and again. Keats, in *Endymion*, would self-consciously reinstate rhyme and couplets in his verse practices, but drew upon the possibilities of the free-flowing verse sentence to develop his own antagonistic approach to verse; rather than pitting line against verse paragraphs, Keats adapted the Akensidean response to Pope by placing sentence and sense at odds with rhymed lines. Wordsworth's blank verse is a more direct successor to Akenside's versification, following a principle of 'guiding' or 'guardianship' wherein the larger structures of metrical verse provide order and organization to the local effects of rhythm and of line. Coleridge too found in Akenside the possibility of thinking seriously and in an open-ended fashion about the structure of the universe and the mind's relation to the world, in and through blank verse.

However direct the debt to Akenside's blank verse in each of Coleridge, Wordsworth, and Keats, all three are united in seeing poetry as a vehicle for philosophizing. This is poetry as a performance of thought, as a kind of dynamic process of 'thinking', as opposed to static communication of 'thought', that Angela Leighton has recently sifted between in the introduction to *Hearing Things*, where Wordsworth is amongst her immediate examples.[118] To this extent, those poets owe much to the eighteenth-century long philosophical poem in general, and much to *Pleasures of Imagination* in particular. Akenside connects Neoclassicism and Romanticism, because each in turn

---

[117] Akenside, *Poetical Works*, p. 87.

[118] Angela Leighton, *Hearing Things: The Work of Sound in Literature* (Cambridge, MA: Harvard University Press, 2018), p. 16.

vitally connects philosophical thinking with verse-form poetry. What should also be kept in view when thinking of Akenside's poetry or other major philosophical poets of the period is that poetry presents a vital alternative to other modes of writing or thinking. Akenside clearly took influence from Joseph Addison's essays, borrowing wholesale the title *Pleasures of Imagination*, and Addison in turn engaged closely with Locke. But Akenside shows a greater debt to Pope, from whom he borrows not title, nor image, nor necessarily individual ideas, but rather a method: of allowing the structures of poetry to shape the structures of thought. Poetry's appearances offer a way of representing the appearances of the world, but also of forming a commentary on the nature of appearances themselves. A pressure applied to semblance unifies the work of Pope, Akenside, Coleridge, Wordsworth, and Keats, and figures as poetry's response to other Enlightenment forms within the long eighteenth century.

Akenside's own works are often give the appearance of a puzzle in that they can at once seem to offer a last flourishing of great Augustan poetry but also a proto-Romantic account of the universe and a pre-emption of Wordsworthian blank verse. The very keyword of the title of Akenside's greatest work – *imagination* – could be and has been called the 'watchword' of Romanticism in general.[119] What of the fact that that watchword is found in the title of an eighteenth-century, Augustan-inspired poem? What this Element has sought to show is that Akenside's poem is not an outlier or aberration in the movements of eighteenth-century poetry, but is instead a vital case study in the continuities that are always present between early and late eighteenth-century verse cultures. It is precisely his role as at once Augustan and early Romantic that should be kept in view as we read Akenside's poetry. This brings us back to connections. The phrase 'philosophic connections' in the title of this work denotes the intermediary role Akenside played in connecting poets as ostensibly different as Pope and Keats. But it also refers to that theoretical approach shared by Pope, Akenside, Coleridge, Wordsworth, and Keats: that poetry might uncover vital connections between the substance of our selves and the worlds around us. Akenside called this the immaterial and material worlds, words culled from then-current empiricist and idealist philosophies, ones that would recur across the breadth of Romanticism. Romanticism might be said to concern, above all else, just such a philosophical connection between spirit and the universe of things. The possibility for glimpsing that connection, as Romanticism learnt from Akenside, is contained in poetry itself: in the fusion of reason and imagination that forms the philosophic poem, in the interplay of thought and

---

[119] Margaret Drabble, ed., *The Oxford Companion to English Literature* (Oxford: Oxford University Press, 1985), p. 843.

feeling, ideas and rhythms that generates new connections in ours minds and forms new connections on the page.

Akenside touches upon just such a theme in Book III of *Pleasures of Imagination*. Writing of the 'mysterious ties' of the 'busy pow'r / Of mem'ry', he reflects on what it means when we think of a past object and then experience once again our past feelings. He is reflecting on the topic that was to be the focus of David Hartley's associationist account of mind, a cornerstone of the philosophical project of the *Lyrical Ballads* and of early Romanticism. Akenside writes:

> Such is the secret union, when we feel
> A song, a flow'r, a name at once restore
> Those long-connected scenes where first they mov'd
> Th'attention; backward thro' her mazy walks
> Guiding the wanton fancy to her scope.
>
> *(III. 338–41).*

We need only add a small French sponge cake to the list of objects and words to appreciate fully its proleptically Proustian theme. Akenside has already warned that too much of a good thing will tend to render that thing less pleasurable – the lesson taken up by Wordsworth in the 'Ode ("There was a time")'. Here he focusses on the opposite idea, the notion that we can make some mental return or backwards movement to the visionary scenes of our past by way of a redemptive associationist habit formed by our memories. This will become, for Akenside, an 'eternal tie':

> For when the diff'rent images of things
> By chance combin'd, have struck th'attentive soul
> With deeper impulse, or connected long,
> Have drawn her frequent eye; howe'er distinct
> Th'external scenes, yet oft th'ideas gain
> From that conjunction an eternal tie,
> And sympathy unbroken.
>
> *(III. 312–18)*

Here, then, is another of the imagination's highest pleasures: the 'unbroken' sense of sympathy that is derived from the chance combination of the images of things. That sense of 'chance' or what he elsewhere calls nature's 'random' blaze, is performed by the ever-shifting nature of the poem's unrhymed lines. But as I have suggested in this Element, verse gives order to even the most varied lines, if those lines pay passing respects to the loose rules of heroic organization. Thus, varied as the verse is, an organizing principle is at work after all.

The poem's philosophical connections, and indeed its philosophy of connectedness, make it so that chance and randomness at the level of line are seen differently at the larger level, as parts of an organized whole; those individual natural phenomena act the same way as we realize all things are connected in God's great plan. Here, then, is a last lesson derived from Pope: whatever *is*, is right, even in its apparently random and disordered make-up. And, as in Pope, the ethical 'sympathetic' notion here recasts contingency as vital necessity. Indeed, the passage just quoted recalls those lines from the start of Pope's *Essay* that introduce the notion of parts containing the whole:

> But of this frame the bearings, and the ties,
> The strong connections, nice dependencies.
>
> *(I. 30–1)*

Here is one of Akenside's favoured terms, 'frame', and here is one of his favourite notions, those 'strong connections' Pope explored between the mind and the world, self and God, part and whole, particular and general, and, ultimately, between ideas and poetic language. All those ideas are met, for Pope as for Akenside, in the relation of appearance to reality. As in *Essay on Man*, *Pleasures of Imagination* tells us that this is how the world seems to be; it concludes that this is also how it must really be. Through the pressure he puts on philosophical appearances, Akenside finally represents a revision of that central argument of *Essay on Man*: whatever *seems to be* is, after all, right.

Bibliography

Abrams, Meyer H. *The Correspondent Breeze* (New York: Norton, 1984).

A Glossary of Literary Terms. 6th ed. (Orlando, FL: Harcourt and Brace, 1993).

Natural Supernaturalism: Tradition and Revolution in Romantic Literature (New York: Norton, 1973).

Addison, Joseph, and Richard Steele (eds.) *The Spectator* (London: 1711–12).

Adorno, Theodor W. *Aesthetic Theory*, Robert Hullot-Kentor (trans.) (London: Continuum, 2004).

Akenside, Mark. *The Poetical Works of Mark Akenside*, Robin Dix (ed.) (Cranbury, NJ: Associated University Presses, 1996).

Attridge, Derek. *The Rhythms of English Poetry* (London: Longman, 1982).

Blake, William. *The Complete Poetry & Prose of William Blake*, David V. Erdman (ed.) (New York: Anchor Books, 1988).

Bloom, Harold. *The Anxiety of Influence: A Theory of Poetry*. 2nd ed. (Oxford: Oxford University Press, 1997).

Bloom, Harold (ed.) *Romanticism and Consciousness* (New York: Norton, 1970).

Buxton, John. *The Grecian Taste: Literature in the Age of Neo-Classicism, 1740–1820* (London: Palgrave, 1978).

Caldwell, James Ralston. *John Keats' Fancy* (Ithaca, NY: Cornell University Press, 1945).

Chandler, James. 'The Pope Controversy: Romantic Poetics and the English Canon', *Critical Inquiry*, vol. 10, no. 3 (1984), pp. 481–509.

Clark, Steve. '"To Bless the Lab'ring Mind": Akenside's *The Pleasures of Imagination*', in Robin Dix (ed.), *Mark Akenside: A Reassessment* (London: Associated University Presses, 2000), pp. 132–52.

Coleridge, Samuel Taylor. *Biographia Literaria*, in H. J. Jackson (ed.), *Samuel Taylor Coleridge: The Major Works* (Oxford: Oxford University Press, 2000).

Collected Letters of Samuel Taylor Coleridge, Earl L. Griggs (ed.), 6 vols. (Oxford: Clarendon, 1956–71).

Lectures 1795 on Politics and Religion, Lewis Patton and Peter Mann (eds.) (Princeton, NJ: Princeton University Press, 1971).

Lectures 1818–1819: On the History of Philosophy, James R. de Jager Jackson (ed.) (Princeton, NJ: Princeton University Press, 2001).

Poems on Various Subjects (Bristol: J. Cottle, 1796).

Poetical Works, Jim C. C. Mays (ed.), 3 vols. (Princeton, NJ: Princeton University Press, 2001).

Table Talk, Carl Woodring (ed.), 2 vols. (Princeton, NJ: Princeton University Press, 1990).

The Watchman, Lewis Patton (ed.) (Princeton, NJ: Princeton University Press, 1970).

Constable, John. 'The Composition and Recomposition of *The Pleasures of Imagination*', in Robin Dix (ed.), *Mark Akenside: A Reassessment* (Cranbury, NJ: Associated University Presses, 2000), pp. 249–83.

Curran, Stuart. *Poetic Form and British Romanticism* (Oxford: Oxford University Press, 1986).

Dennis, John. *Reflections Critical and Satyrical, Upon a Late Rhapsody Call'd, An Essay Upon Criticism* (London: B. Lintott, 1711).

Dix, Robin. *The Literary Career of Mark Akenside* (Cranbury, NJ: Associated University Presses, 2006).

Mark Akenside: A Reassessment (Cranbury, NJ: Associated University Presses, 2000).

Drabble, Margaret (ed.) *The Oxford Companion to English Literature* (Oxford: Oxford University Press, 1985).

Engell, James. *The Creative Imagination* (Cambridge, MA: Harvard University Press, 1981).

Fabel, Kirk M. 'The Location of the Aesthetic in Akenside's *Pleasures of Imagination*', *Philological Quarterly*, vol. 76, no. 1 (1997), 47–68.

Freer, Alexander. 'Rhythm As Coping', *New Literary History*, vol. 46, no. 3 (2015), 549–68.

Fry, Paul H. *Theory of Poetry* (New Haven, CT: Yale University Press, 2012).

Fussell, Paul. *Poetic Meter and Poetic Form* (New York: Random House, 1965).

Groves, Peter L. *Strange Music: The Metre of the English Heroic Line* (Victoria, BC: University of Victoria [English Literary Studies], 1998).

Hartman, Geoffrey H. 'Inscriptions and Romantic Nature Poetry', in *The Unremarkable Wordsworth* (London: Methuen, 1987), pp. 31–46.

'Reflections on the Evening Star: Akenside to Coleridge', in Geoffrey H. Hartman (ed.), *New Perspectives on Coleridge and Wordsworth* (Columbia, NY: Columbia University Press, 1972), pp. 85–93.

Wordsworth's Poetry, 1787–1814 (New Haven, CT: Yale University Press, 1964).

Hegel, Georg Wilhelm Friedrich. *Hegel's Aesthetics: Lectures on Fine Arts*, Thomas Malcolm Knox (trans.), 2 vols. (Oxford: Clarendon, 1988).

Hume, David. *An Enquiry Concerning Human Understanding*, Eric Steinberg (ed.) (Indianapolis, IN: Hackett, 1993).

Hunt, Leigh. *The Examiner*, 292 (London: 1817).

Hunter, J. Paul. 'Form As Meaning: Pope and the Ideology of the Couplet Form', *The Eighteenth Century*, vol. 37, no. 3 (1996), pp. 257–70.

Jacobus, Mary. *Tradition and Experiment in Wordsworth's Lyrical Ballads (1798)* (Oxford: Clarendon, 1976).

Jarvis, Simon. 'Bedlam or Parnassus: The Verse Idea', *Metaphilosophy*, vol. 43, no. 1–2 (2012), 71–81.

'Thinking in Verse', in James Chandler (ed.), *The Cambridge Companion to British Romantic Poetry* (Cambridge: Cambridge University Press, 2008), pp. 98–116.

Wordsworth's Philosophic Song (Cambridge: Cambridge University Press, 2007).

Johnson, Samuel. *The Works of Samuel Johnson, LL.D.*, John Hawkins (ed.), 11 vols. (Cambridge: Cambridge University Press, 2011).

Jones, Tom. 'Argumentative Emphases in Pope's *An Essay on Man*', in Joanna Fowler and Allan Ingram (eds.), *Voice and Context in Eighteenth-Century Verse: Order in Variety* (London: Palgrave, 2015), pp. 47–63.

Pope and Berkeley: The Language of Poetry and Philosophy (London: Palgrave, 2005).

Jump, Harriet. 'High Sentiments of Liberty: Coleridge's Unacknowledged Debt to Akenside', *Studies in Romanticism*, vol. 28, no. 2 (1989), 207–24.

'"That Other Eye": Wordsworth's 1794 Revisions of "An Evening Walk"', *The Wordsworth Circle*, vol. 17, no. 3 (1986), 156–63.

Kant, Immanuel. *Critique of the Power of Judgment*, Paul Guyer (ed.) (Cambridge: Cambridge University Press, 2000).

Keats, John. *Keats's Poetry and Prose*, Jeffrey N. Cox (ed.) (New York: Norton, 2009).

Kenner, Hugh. 'Pope's Reasonable Rhymes', *ELH*, vol. 41, no. 1 (1974), 74–88.

Kitching, Megan. '"When Universal Nature I Survey": Philosophical Poetry before 1750', in Joanna Fowler and Allan Ingram (eds.), *Voice and Context in Eighteenth-Century Verse: Order in Variety* (London: Palgrave, 2015), pp. 83–100.

Knox-Shaw, Peter. 'Unseen Stars: Addison, Akenside, Young, and Huygens', *ANQ*, vol. 32, no. 4 (2019), 227–30.

Leibnitz, Gottfried Wilhelm. *Essays of Theodicy on the Goodness of God, the Freedom of Man and the Origin of Evil* (Chicago, IL: Open Court, 1999).

Leighton, Angela. *Hearing Things: The Work of Sound in Literature* (Cambridge, MA: Harvard University Press, 2018).

Locke, John. *An Essay Concerning Human Understanding*, Peter Nidditch (ed.) (Oxford: Clarendon, 1979).

Lau, Beth. 'Poetic Precursors (2): Spenser, Milton, Dryden, Pope', in Michael O' Neill (ed.), *John Keats in Context* (Cambridge University Press, 2017), pp. 220–8.

Mack, Maynard (ed.) *The Last and Greatest Art: Some Unpublished Poetical Manuscripts of Alexander Pope* (Newark: University of Delaware Press, 1984).

'On Reading Pope', *College English*, vol. 7, no. 5 (1946), pp. 263–73.

Mahoney, John L. 'Addison and Akenside: The Impact of Psychological Criticism on Early English Romantic Poetry', *The British Journal of Aesthetics*, vol. 6, no. 4 (1966), 365–74.

Marsh, Robert. 'Akenside and Addison: The Problem of Ideational Debt', *Modern Philology*, vol. 59, no. 1 (1961), 36–48.

Maxwell, Ian R. 'Beauty Is Truth', *Journal of the Australasian Universities Language and Literature Association*, vol. 10, no. 1 (1959), 100–9.

McGann, Jerome J. *The Romantic Ideology* (Chicago, IL: University of Chicago Press, 1983).

Nietzsche, Friedrich. *The Birth of Tragedy and Other Writings*, Raymond Geuss and Ronald Speirs (eds.) (Cambridge: Cambridge University Press, 1999).

Norton, John. 'Akenside's *The Pleasures of Imagination*: An Exercise in Poetics', *Eighteenth-Century Studies*, vol. 3, no. 3 (1970), 366–83.

Perry, Seamus. 'Wordsworth's Heroics', *The Wordsworth Circle*, vol. 34, no. 2 (2003), 65–73.

Pope, Alexander. *An Essay on Man*, Tom Jones (ed.) (Princeton, NJ: Princeton University Press, 2016).

Pound, Ezra. *Make It New* (New Haven, CT: Yale University Press, 1935).

Reid, Nicholas. 'Coleridge, Akenside, and the Platonic Tradition: Reading in *The Pleasures of Imagination*', *Journal of Language, Literature, and Culture*, vol. 80, no. 1 (1993), 31–56.

Rogers, Pat. *Essays on Pope* (Cambridge: Cambridge University Press, 1993).

Rollins, Hyder Edwards (ed.) *The Keats Circle: Letters and Papers* (Cambridge, MA: Harvard University Press, 1965).

Rorty, Richard. *Philosophy and the Mirror of Nature* (Princeton, NJ: Princeton University Press, 1979).

Saintsbury, George. *A History of English Prosody from the Twelfth Century to the Present Day*, 4 vols. (London: Macmillan, 1906).

Sha, Richard C. 'Toward a Physiology of the Romantic Imagination', *Configurations*, vol. 17, no. 3 (2009), 197–226.

Shelley, Percy Bysshe. *Shelley's Poetry and Prose*, Donald H. Reiman and Neil Freistat (ed.) (New York: Norton, 2002), 37–48.

Sitter, John E. 'Pope's Versification and Voice', *The Cambridge Companion to Alexander Pope*, Pat Rogers (ed.) (Cambridge: Cambridge University Press, 2007).

'Theodicy at Midcentury: Young, Akenside, Hume', *Eighteenth-Century Studies*, vol. 12, no. 1 (1978), 90–106.

Solomon, Harry M. *The Rape of the Text: Reading and Misreading Pope's* Essay on Man (Tuscaloosa: University of Alabama Press, 1993).

Sowerby, Robin. *The Augustan Art of Poetry* (Oxford: Oxford University Press, 2006).

Stewart, Dustin D. 'Akenside's Refusal of Allegory: *The Pleasures of Imagination* (1744)', *Journal for Eighteenth-Century Studies*, vol. 34, no. 3 (2011), 315–33.

Stock, Robin D. *The Holy and the Daemonic from Sir Thomas Browne to William Blake* (Princeton, NJ: Princeton University Press, 1982).

Townsend, Chris. 'Nature and the Language of the Sense: Berkeley's Thought in Coleridge and Wordsworth', *Romanticism*, vol. 25, no. 2 (2019), 129–42.

Vallins, David. 'Akenside, Coleridge, and the Pleasures of Transcendence', *Mark Akenside: A Reassessment*, Robin Dix (ed.) (Cranbury, NJ: Associated University Presses, 2000), 156–82.

Warton, Joseph, *Essay on the Genius and Writings of Pope*, vol. 1 (London: M. Cooper, 1756).

Essay on the Genius and Writings of Pope, vol. 2 (London: T. Maiden, 1782).

Weinbrot, Howard D., *Alexander Pope and the Traditions of Formal Verse Satire* (Princeton, NJ: Princeton University Press, 1982).

Wimsatt Jr, W. K, and M. C. Beardsley. 'The Intentional Fallacy', *The Sewanee Review*, vol. 54, no. 3 (1946), 468–88.

Wordsworth, William. *The Major Works*, Stephen Gill (ed.) (Oxford: Oxford University Press, 2008).

The Poetical Works of William Wordsworth, Ernest De Selincourt and Helen Darbishire (eds.), 5 vols. (Oxford: Clarendon, 1940–9).

Acknowledgements

This work was completed with the generous support of a Residential Research Library Fellowship at Durham University in 2019. My fellowship in particular enabled me to make full use of the Robin Dix Akenside Collection held by the university library with its unparalleled catalogue of rare and first editions of Akenside's work. I owe thanks to the organizers of Durham's fellowships, but also to the late Robin Dix; it is on the impressive shoulders of his scholarship that the current Ele,emt stands.

Thanks also due to Ned Allen and Sophie Read at Christ's College, University of Cambridge, and to Tom Jones at the University of St Andrews.

Cambridge Elements ☰

Eighteenth-Century Connections

Series Editors

Eve Tavor Bannet
University of Oklahoma

Eve Tavor Bannet is George Lynn Cross Professor Emeritus, University of Oklahoma and editor of *Studies in Eighteenth-Century Culture*. Her monographs include *Empire of Letters: Letter Manuals and Transatlantic Correspondence 1688–1820* (Cambridge, 2005), *Transatlantic Stories and the History of Reading, 1720–1820* (Cambridge, 2011), and *Eighteenth-Century Manners of Reading: Print Culture and Popular Instruction in the Anglophone Atlantic World* (Cambridge, 2017). She is editor of *British and American Letter Manuals 1680–1810* (Pickering & Chatto, 2008), *Emma Corbett* (Broadview, 2011) and, with Susan Manning, *Transatlantic Literary Studies* (Cambridge, 2012).

Rebecca Bullard
University of Reading

Rebecca Bullard is Associate Professor of English Literature at the University of Reading. She is the author of *The Politics of Disclosure: Secret History Narratives, 1674–1725* (Pickering & Chatto, 2009), co-editor of *The Plays and Poems of Nicholas Rowe, volume 1* (Routledge, 2017) and co-editor of *The Secret History in Literature, 1660–1820* (Cambridge, 2017).

Advisory Board

Linda Bree, Independent
Claire Connolly, University College Cork
Gillian Dow, University of Southampton
James Harris, University of St Andrews
Thomas Keymer, University of Toronto
Jon Mee, University of York
Carla Mulford, Penn State University
Nicola Parsons, University of Sydney
Manushag Powell, Purdue University
Robbie Richardson, University of Kent
Shef Rogers, University of Otago
Eleanor Shevlin, West Chester University
David Taylor, Oxford University
Chloe Wigston Smith, University of York
Roxann Wheeler, Ohio State University
Eugenia Zuroski, MacMaster University

About the Series

Exploring connections between verbal and visual texts and the people, networks, cultures and places that engendered and enjoyed them during the long Eighteenth Century, this innovative series also examines the period's uses of oral, written and visual media, and experiments with the digital platform to facilitate communication of original scholarship with both colleagues and students.

Cambridge Elements ☰

Eighteenth-Century Connections

Elements in the Series

Voltaire's Correspondence: Digital Readings
Nicholas Cronk and Glenn Roe

Mary Prince, Slavery, and Print Culture in the Anglophone Atlantic World
Juliet Shields

Disavowing Disability: Richard Baxter and the Conditions of Salvation
Andrew McKendry

How and Why to Do Things with Eighteenth-Century Manuscripts
Michelle Levy and Betty A. Schellenberg

Philosophical Connections: Akenside, Neoclassicism, Romanticism
Chris Townsend